WRITER-FILES

General Editor: Simon Trussler

Associate Editor: Malcolm Page

File on
SYNGE

Compiled by Nesta Jones

Methuen Drama

A Methuen Drama Book

First published in Great Britain 1994
by Methuen Drama,
an imprint of Reed Consumer Books Ltd.,
Michelin House, 81 Fulham Road, London SW3 6RB,
and Auckland, Melbourne, Singapore, and Toronto,
and distributed in the United States of America by HEB Inc.,
361 Hanover Street, Portsmouth, New Hampshire 03801-3959

EG18549

ISBN 0 413 65630 6

A CIP catalogue record for this book
is available at the British Library

Typeset in 9/10 Times
by Country Setting,
Woodchurch, Kent TN26 3TB

Printed in Great Britain
by Cox and Wyman Ltd.,
Cardiff Road, Reading

Front cover portrait
of J. M. Synge (1905) by J. B. Yeats.
Reproduced by courtesy of
the National Gallery of Ireland

Contents

Acknowledgements

I should like to thank the following for their
assistance during the preparation of this volume:
Pauline Ryall, Goldsmiths' College Library,
University of London; Tim O'Neill, former
Director of the Project Arts Centre, Dublin;
Anne O'Callaghan, Press Officer, Abbey
Theatre, Dublin; Jane Daly and Anne Butler,
Druid Theatre Company, Galway;
Ruth Molyneux, West Yorkshire Playhouse;
the Press Office of the Royal National Theatre
of Great Britain; the Press Office of the Citizens'
Theatre, Glasgow; the Archivist of the Synge
Manuscripts, Trinity College Library, Dublin;
Wan-Jae Jang; Noël Sidebottom, National Sound
Archive; and Dominic Jones, Pinnacle Records.

My particular thanks also go to
Christopher Sanderson for his invaluable
help during the initial research and to
Brenda Ford for her expertise and patience
in processing the typescript.

For my son and in memory of my mother.

The theatre is, by its nature, an ephemeral art: yet it is a daunting task to track down the newspaper reviews, or contemporary statements from the writer or his director, which are often all that remain to help us recreate some sense of what a particular production was like. This series is therefore intended to make readily available a selection of the comments that the critics made about the plays of leading modern dramatists at the time of their production — and to trace, too, the course of each writer's own views about his work and his world.

In addition to combining a uniquely convenient source of such elusive *documentation*, the 'Writer-Files' series also assembles the *information* necessary for readers to pursue further their interest in a particular writer or work. Variations in quantity between one writer's output and another's, differences in temperament which make some readier than others to talk about their work, and the variety of critical response, all mean that the presentation and balance of material shifts between one volume and another: but we have tried to arrive at a format for the series which will nevertheless enable users of one volume readily to find their way around any other.

Section 1, 'A Brief Chronology', provides a quick conspective overview of each playwright's life and career. *Section 2* deals with the plays themselves, arranged chronologically in the order of their composition: information on first performances, major revivals, and publication is followed by a brief synopsis (for quick reference set in slightly larger, italic type), then by a representative selection of the critical response, and of the dramatist's own comments on the play and its theme.

Section 3 offers concise guidance to each writer's work in non-dramatic forms, while *Section 4*, 'The Writer on His Work', brings together comments from the playwright himself on more general matters of construction, opinion, and artistic development. Finally, *Section 5* provides a bibliographical guide to other primary and secondary sources of further reading, among which full details will be found of works cited elsewhere under short titles, and of collected editions of the plays — but not of individual titles, particulars of which will be found with the other factual data in Section 2.

The 'Writer-Files' hope by striking this kind of balance between information and a wide range of opinion to offer 'companions' to the study of major playwrights in the modern repertoire — not in that dangerous pre-digested fashion which can too readily quench the desire to read the plays themselves, nor so prescriptively as to allow any single line of approach to predominate, but rather to encourage readers to form their own judgements of the plays in a wide-ranging context.

J. M. Synge had the good fortune and the ill fortune to be a highly individual genius who was both encouraged and entrapped by an irresistibly collective historic moment — a veritable renaissance, as that spurt of directed energy in Irish culture early in the present century has been insistently described. Without its ambience he would, perhaps, never have turned to the drama: within it, the tensions between his own creative drive and the needs of his society were pervasive.

And so, as the programme note to the Abbey's 1988 revival (reprinted on page 82) suggests, we should not 'look down too haughtily' on the playgoers who, during the *Playboy* riots, were sensitive not only to mentions of female undergarments but also to evidence of that 'stage Irishness' through which British cultural and colonial hegemony expressed itself in contempt for stereotyped 'natives'. Indeed, as several items in this collection affirm, Synge created a no less artificial if by intention more sympathetic version of 'stage Irishness': thus, citing the work of Nicholas Grene, John Barber maintains on page 76 that Synge's dialogue is 'faked' — 'based on authentic speech', but coloured to satisfy 'a middle-class urban audience to whom peasant life was unfamiliar and romantic — as, to a degree, it was to Synge'. The creation of this highly theatrical yet synthetic dialect may, as Barber suggests, make Synge a superior artist: but it distanced him from the reality which naturalism was attempting to embrace, as also from the folkloric truth which many of his compatriots preferred. He becomes a writer in whose work we are, 'just as at the opera . . . enmeshed by the tunes and harmonies'.

Even allowing the corrective force of this view, one comes away from the documentation here assembled with increased respect for a writer who, in the face of the ill health which dogged his creative prime, still managed to attend assiduously to the business of the theatre, to keep in touch with the broader cultural scene of London and the continental capitals, to pay his regular visits of homage and of renewal to the Aran Islands — and to seek for a personal love that remained ever elusive. No wonder that, as Jack Kroll observes on page 74, Synge created 'the earthy and divine rant of creatures who have to fabricate a glory to counteract the onerous reality of their lives' — a point affirmed, of *The Well of the Saints*, by no less an authority than Yeats, who declares (on page 45) that it is the preoccupation of Synge's characters 'with their dream that gives his plays their drifting movement, their emotional subtlety' — 'a simple motive lifted, as it were, into the full light of the stage'.

Simon Trussler

1871 16 April, born at 2 Newtown Villas, Rathfarnham, County Dublin, youngest of eight children, three of whom died in infancy. His father, John Hatch Synge, a barrister, came from a well-known Wicklow family; his mother, Kathleen, was the daughter of the Protestant rector of Schull in County Cork, a classical scholar and evangelical zealot.

1872 Death of his father. Mrs. Synge moves to Orwell Park in the suburb of Rathgar, to live next door to her mother. Synge lives here until he is twenty.

1881 Attends Mr. Harrick's Classical and English School in Dublin with his brother Samuel.

1884 Briefly at Aravon House School, Bray. For the next four years is tutored privately three times a week. Spends summers regularly in County Wicklow. Suffers from asthma, which was to plague him throughout his life. Enjoys walking and fishing with elder brothers, Robert and Edward, but spends most of his time with Samuel and his cousin Florence Ross, who lives next door, both of whom share his interest in natural history. Reads Darwin and rejects the evangelical teaching of his mother and grandmother.

1886 Joins Dublin Naturalists' Field Club. Moves slowly away from the social, religious, and political beliefs of his family. By the mid-1880s, Robert has gone to Argentina, Edward is a land agent for the family estates in County Wicklow and other properties in the West of Ireland, and his sister Annie has married a solicitor.

1887 Oct., takes violin lessons, and develops an interest in Irish antiquities.

1888 Accepted by Trinity College, Dublin, and starts studying in Feb. the following year.

1889 Nov., enrols in the Royal Irish Academy of Music to study the violin, composition, and musical theory.

1890 Scrapes a third-class result in the first-year exams at Trinity, and is certified by the Academy to pursue advanced study in counterpoint. Moves with his mother to 31 Crosthwaite Park, Kingstown (now Dun Laoghaire), next door to his sister, brother-in-law and their three children. His brother Samuel prepares for a career as a medical missionary in China.

1891 Florence's mother dies; she joins the Synge household. Synge refuses to attend church services, which further alienates him from family.

1892 Pursues his interests in music, languages, walking, and cycling. Joins the student orchestra at the Academy and wins prizes in harmony and counterpoint. Studies German and takes classes in Hebrew and Irish at Trinity, winning prizes in both languages. Dec., awarded second-class degree from Trinity. Continues his studies at the Academy, begins to write an opera, and joins the Dublin Junior Instrumental club. W. B. Yeats founds the Irish Literary Society in Dublin. Douglas Hyde addresses the Society on 'The De-Anglicization of Ireland', which leads to the formation of the Gaelic League, dedicated to restoring the old Gaelic culture and language.

1893 Mary Synge, his father's cousin and a professional musician, visits Dublin. She holds a piano recital in the Ancient Concert Rooms, organized by Synge. Mary persuades Mrs. Synge to allow her son to study music in Germany and he resumes his studies in German. 25 July, leaves Dublin with Mary Synge. 29 July, arrives in Oberwerth, an island in the Rhine near Koblenz, where he stays at a guest house run by the six Von Eicken sisters. 7 Oct., Mary Synge returns to London, leaving Synge at Oberwerth where he studies German literature, the violin (with Konrad Henbuer), and plays with the local orchestral society. Valeska, one of the Von Eicken sisters, becomes his close confidante.

1894 22 Jan., moves to Wurzburg to continue musical studies in the piano. Records in diaries in April and May that he is attempting to write poetry and a play in German. Goes to Frankfurt to visit the birthplace of Goethe, whose work he is studying. 14 June, returns to Dublin, joins his mother in County Wicklow. July-Aug., among the house-party is Cherrie Matheson, a neighbour from Crosthwaite Park and sketching companion to Florence, with whom Synge falls in love. 3 Nov.-31 Dec., stays in Oberwerth studying German and French.

1895 1 Jan., arrives in Paris. Joins the Société Fraternelle d'Étudiants Protestants; attends lectures at the Sorbonne and the École Pratique des Hautes-Études; participates in cultural and recreational activities in and around Paris; some of his attempts to write regularly about public events in France for Irish readers published anonymously in the *Irish Times*. Continues his serious study of literature, and, on returning to Dublin on 28 June, resolves to be a writer. Resumes his relationship with Cherrie, accompanying her to exhibitions in Dublin (she exhibited at the Paris Salon). Throughout Nov. and Dec. takes lessons in Italian in preparation for a visit the following year.

1896 3 Jan.-3 Feb., in Paris, at Hôtel Corneille: continues his study of French (with Thérèse Beydon) and Italian; attends theatre regularly; meets Dr. James Cree (another Dubliner). Travels to Rome where he stays till 30 April. Enrols in literature courses at Collegio Romano. Writes newspaper reports on riots and demonstrations over the failure of the Italian invasion of Abyssinia. May, in Florence, meets Maria Antoinette Zdanowska, a Polish student of sculpture and devout Roman Catholic (subsequently meets often in Paris) and Hope Rea, an English art historian and theosophist, with whom he corresponds for the rest of his life. June, returns to Paris; corresponds with Cherrie, proposing marriage on 3 June, by letter. Her refusal arrives on 17 June. Synge continues courtship for next two years. 29 June, leaves for Ireland joining mother in County Wicklow. 27-28 Oct., visits Hope Rea in London on his way back to Paris, where he studies socialism. At Hôtel Corneille continues to write anonymously for the *Irish Times*; studies at the Sorbonne (courses in Petrarch, La Fontaine), sees James Cree frequently, and meets Stephen MacKenna. 21 Dec., meets William Butler Yeats and 27 Dec., Maud Gonne.

1897 At lodgings in Rue Léopold-Robert. Continues his studies with Thérèse Beydon and joins weekly debating society. 1 Jan., at inaugural meeting of Association Irlandaise founded by Yeats and Maud Gonne. He draws up the list of associate members and becomes heavily involved with the organization; however, he resigns from the Association when he becomes suspicious of Maud Gonne's political motives, although he continues to attend weekly meetings. Establishes a close relationship with Stephen MacKenna (another independent but impoverished Irishman); writes series of impressionistic essays which only MacKenna is allowed to read; attends lectures on moral action, feminism, and the Breton revival with MacKenna and James Cree. 13 May, returns to Dublin. Pursues Irish interests: joins Yeats and Maud Gonne at the Contemporary Club, meets George Russell (AE), with whom he attends meetings of the Theosophical Society. Spends summer in Wicklow, trying unsuccessfully to meet Cherrie Matheson. 31 Aug., back in Dublin, but delays his return to Paris due to swollen glands in his neck – first indication of Hodgkin's disease, which would eventually kill him. 11 Dec., undergoes surgery; writes an essay on the experience under ether.

1898 19 Jan., leaves Dublin for London, drawing £60 from his principal and wearing a black wig to cover his temporary baldness, caused by the operation. Two days in London visiting Hope Rea and Yeats. Returns to Paris: increases his circle of Irish friends with Richard Best, introduced to him by MacKenna; also meets Margaret Hardon, an American etcher and student of architecture, to whom he is attracted. 27 April, returns to Dublin. 10 May, first visit to the Aran Islands; stays at Atlantic Hotel on Inishmore for two weeks, then travels to Inishmaan, where he stays with Patrick McDonagh, whose son Martin becomes his tutor. Lives in a cottage on mackerel and eggs, learning Irish. 27 June, Yeats invites him to Lady Gregory's home at Coole Park. 28 June, stays with Edward Martyn at Tullirra Castle. 29 June, returns to Kingstown. 'A Story from Inishmaan' is published in the November issue of *New Ireland Review*. 18 Nov., returns to Paris, taking a room in 90 Rue d'Assas, which was to be his home for the next five years. 17 Dec., his review of Maeterlinck's *La Sagesse et la Destinée* appears in the *Dublin Daily Express*. Begins article on the Breton writer Anatole Le Braz. During the year Yeats, Lady Gregory, and Edward Martyn declare, in a manifesto, their intention to found an Irish Literary Theatre. This is formally done at a meeting of the Council of the National Literary Society on 16 Jan. the following year.

1899 28 Jan., the Le Braz article appears in the *Dublin Daily Express*. 31 Jan.-16 Feb., Yeats in Paris, meets with Synge frequently. Continues to study Breton language, and 3-16 April goes to Quimper with Breton friend, Dr. Piquenard. The results of this experience appear in essay form the following year ('A Celtic Theatre', *Freeman's Journal*, 22 Mar. 1900). Continues to see Maud Gonne, Maria Zdanowska, and Margaret Hardon. 8 May, returns to Dublin. 12 May, attends Irish Literary Theatre production of *The Countess Cathleen* (Yeats) and *The Heather Field* (Edward Martyn). 1 June, arrives at Castle Kevin, County Wicklow, for summer stay; in the house-party is Edie Harmar (sister to Samuel's wife, Mary), with whom he develops a lasting friendship. Corresponds regularly with Thérèse Beydon and Margaret Hardon, who deflects his romantic overtures. 12 Sept.-7 Oct., second visit to Aran. Afterwards spends two weeks in Dublin at the Contemporary Club, where he associates with Yeats's friends and Dublin's best talkers. 20 Oct., his brother Robert returns from South America. 3 Nov., returns to Paris.

1900 April, Lady Gregory, in Paris, encourages Synge to continue his Aran Islands articles and suggests Jack B. Yeats as a possible illustrator. 24 May, returns to Dublin, attends Gaelic League's music festival, Feis Coeil; leaves for Castle Kevin on 1 June. The house-party includes Annie Harmar (another of Sam's sisters-in-laws) and Rosie L. Calthrop (a cousin of the Harmars) with whom Synge immediately establishes a rapport; Edie Harmar joins the household when Rosie departs. 15 Sept.-

14 Oct., third visit to Aran Islands, staying with the McDonaghs on Inishmaan. Before leaving for Paris on 31 Oct., Synge buys a typewriter. Once again troubled by enlarged glands at the back of his neck.

1901 This condition continues to trouble him; a Russian doctor advises him to have the glands removed. Another Aran essay, 'The Last Fortress of the Gael', is published in the April issue of the New York *Gael*. 6 May, returns to Dublin, where he receives treatment from his doctor (Dr. Parsons). 3 June, joins party at Castle Kevin which includes Rose Calthrop. 14-20 Sept., at Coole with Yeats and Lady Gregory. They discuss his first play *When the Moon Has Set* and his manuscript (to date) of *The Aran Islands*. 2 Sept.-9 Oct., on Inishmaan and Inishere, taking violin with him. 21 Oct., attends third and final season of the Irish Literary Theatre, seeing *Diarmund and Grania* by Yeats and George Moore and the first play in Irish in a professional theatre, *Casadh an Tsugain*, by Douglas Hyde, under the direction of W. G. Fay. 1 Nov., attends Lady Gregory's 'at home' in London and an exhibition of paintings by Jack B. Yeats. 26 Nov., leaves for Paris submitting his Aran manuscript to Grant Richards in London en route.

1902 Despite suffering from influenza and the rejections of his book, he continues to work on his Wicklow articles. Jan., commissioned by *L'European* to write 'La Vieille Litterature Irlandaise', on Irish literature, for March issue; also studies old Irish with Professor d'Arbois de Jubainville at the Sorbonne. Cree leaves Paris and MacKenna prepares for his marriage. His new companion is his cousin Edward Synge, an etcher. Begins work on two verse plays. 17 May, returns to Ireland, reviews Lady Gregory's *Cuchulain of Muirthemme* and Seamus MacMeanus's *Donegal Fairy Stories* for *The Speaker* (7 and 21 June respectively). 21 July-6 Sept., at Tomriland House, near Castle Kevin. Synge completes *Riders to the Sea* and *In the Shadow of the Glen,* and starts work on *The Tinker's Wedding*. Mrs. Synge employs a new cook, Eileen; he recalls her hearty laugh and witty exchanges with the workmen below his bedroom window in the preface to *The Playboy of the Western World*. 6 Sept., two articles published, 'The Old and New in Ireland' in *Academy and Literature* and a review of Geoffrey Keating's *History of Ireland* in *The Speaker*. 8-11 Oct., at Coole, discussing his plays and Aran book with Yeats and Lady Gregory. The Irish National Dramatic Company, an amateur organization of considerable repute run by William G. Fay and his brother Frank, joins forces with the Irish Literary Theatre: this combination was to become the Irish National Theatre Society. 14 Oct.-8 Nov., on Inishere. 14 Nov., meets Clare von Eicken in Dublin. 23 Nov., Cherrie Matheson marries. 4 Dec., visits Camden Street Theatre to see Fay brothers' company in F. J. Ryan's *The*

Laying of the Foundations, Yeats and Lady Gregory's *The Pot of Broth*, and *Eilís agus an Bhean Deírce*, by Peadar MacFhionnlaich. Lady Gregory introduces him to James Joyce, who seeks assistance in planning his journey to Paris.

1903 10 Jan., in London. Yeats introduces him to the literary circle attending his Monday 'at home' in Woburn Buildings (John Masefield, Arthur Symons, G. K. Chesterton, Pamela Colman Smith, Florence Farr). Lady Gregory publicizes his plays to literary friends and publishers. Commissioned by J. L. Hammond of *The Speaker* to provide occasional articles on contemporary French literature (18 April, first of these appears on Loti, Anatole France, and Huysmans), and sees publisher Brinsley Johnson about his Aran manuscript. 6 Nov., returns to Paris to remove belongings from his room in the Rue d'Assas. Meets Joyce in Paris on several occasions at the bistro-restaurant in the Rue Saint-André-des-Arts. *Fortnightly* rejects *Riders to the Sea*. 12 March, bids farewell to Thérèse Beydon and leaves Paris for the last time. 18 March, returns to Ireland, where Fay's company has accepted *In the Shadow of the Glen* for performance in the autumn by the Irish National Theatre Society. April, 'An Autumn in the Hills' published in the New York *Gael*. Rescues *Riders to the Sea* for Fay and reduces first play, *When the Moon Has Set*, to one act. Spends early part of the summer in touch with rehearsals in Camden Street. 28 Aug.-19 Sept., visits County Kerry for the first time. Yeats publishes *Riders to the Sea* in Oct. issue of *Samhain* (journal of the Irish Literary Society). 8 Oct., first production of *In the Shadow of the Glen* in a double bill with Yeats's *The King's Threshold*. The *Irish Independent* describes both plays in advance as 'unwholesome productions'. Dudley Diggs, an actor in Fay's company since its inception, refuses to perform and resigns from the Society. On the opening night Diggs, his wife, and Maud Gonne walk out of the performance. Maud Gonne attacks the Society in the *United Irishman*, commenting on 'foreign thoughts and philosophies'. The most far-reaching accusations come from Arthur Griffith (founder of Sinn Fein), the editor of the *United Irishman*. Both Yeats and his father write in Synge's defence, but the controversy continues for several weeks. 17 Oct., the plays are given repeat performances; Synge elected to membership of the reading committee of the Society. Frequently attends rehearsals, but prevented from seeing subsequent production due to ill health; during convalescence composes first drafts of his unfinished farce *National Drama*, and more serious poetic drama, *The Lady O'Conor*.

1904 Regularly attends rehearsals of the Society's productions. Meticulously prepares for a production of *Riders to the Sea*, writing to Galway for cloth and the Aran Islands for pampooties (traditional Aran footwear). 25 Feb., Synge attends opening of *Riders to the Sea,* despite severe toothache and accompanying fever; the play receives largely unfavourable reviews. March, 'A Dream of Inishmaan' published in the New York *Gael.* 26 March, Synge travels with players to London for matinee performance of *Riders* and *Shadow* at the Court Theatre: plays receive almost unanimous acclaim, with excellent reviews from William Archer and Max Beerbohm. Yeats introduces him to the designer Charles Ricketts; commissioned by the editor of *Academy and Literature* to contribute Irish entries for the unsigned 'Literary Notes' section. His responsibility to the Society increases, reading and revising plays. Frank Fay encourages him to begin a scenario on the 1798 rebellion, but this is met with little enthusiasm from his colleagues. 7 June, Samuel and his family return from China. 17 June, Frank Fay reads *Well of the Saints* to the company. 16 July, at Coole Park assisting Lady Gregory with revisions of her play *Kincora.* 1 Aug.-1 Sept., in Kerry; proposed visit to Aran cancelled due to typhus epidemic on the islands. 17 Sept., begins two week cycle tour of North Mayo. 10 Oct., attends rehearsals of *Well of the Saints* in Camden Street; takes rooms at 15 Maxwell Road, Rathgar, to be nearer to the centre of Dublin. Influenced by Yeats, Lady Gregory, and AE, he turns once again to psychic exploration. 12 Nov., his review of Fiona Macleod's *The Winged Destiny* in *Academy and Literature.* Miss Annie Horniman offers the Society a permanent home in what was to become the Abbey Theatre. 31 Oct., American lawyer, John Quinn, present with Synge at rehearsals in the new theatre; when *The Shadow of the Glen* is published in *Samhain* in Dec., Quinn arranges for a copyright edition in New York. 27 Dec., Abbey Theatre opens.

1905 Jan., Synge conducts rehearsals of *The Well of the Saints,* which opens on 4 Feb. 'An Impression of Aran' and 'The Oppression of the Hills' published in the *Manchester Guardian* (24 Jan. and 15 Feb. respectively). Arthur Griffith revives his attack on Synge and Yeats and the source of *The Shadow of the Glen* in *The United Irishman.* Yeats rejoins, causing a lengthy argument which extends over several weeks; a letter from Synge affirming his source in the Aran Islands was finally published. Privately, Synge sketches several scenarios on the theme of 'Deaf Mutes for Ireland', and he and Yeats even consider publishing Synge's farce *National Drama* in retaliation. *The Well of the Saints* is hardly a critical or popular success, but brings Synge to the attention of continental theatres. The Frenchman Henry Lebeau and Breton writer Anatole Le Braz visit Ireland. Lebeau's article praising *The Well of the Saints* is simultaneously published in Paris and Dublin. George Moore sends the article to the German translator Dr. Max Meyerfeld, who immediately writes for permission to translate the play. Meanwhile

Karel Musek of the Bohemian National Theatre in Prague requests permission to translate *The Shadow of the Glen*. 15 Feb., Synge moves back to Crosthwaite Park to live with his mother, who has been ill for some time. April, sits for John Butler Yeats, who has been commissioned by Hugh Lane to paint portraits of all the leaders of the literary revival. May, a week in Donegal fishing with brother Edward. 8 May, Elkin Matthews publishes *The Shadow of the Glen* and *Riders to the Sea*. Commissioned by the *Manchester Guardian* to write a series of articles on the west of Ireland with Jack B. Yeats as illustrator. 3 June-3 July, the two men travel north from Galway, through Connemara and Mayo. 10 June-26 July, twelve articles appear in the paper. George Roberts, managing director of the newly established publishers Maunsel and Company, seeks permission to publish the articles as a book (a project which was realized after Synge's death). Roberts persuades Synge to retrieve the *Aran* manuscript from Matthews, giving publishing rights to Maunsel. 7 Aug., returns to Kerry, where he crosses to the Blasket Islands. Supported by Miss Horniman and the Fay Brothers, Yeats and Lady Gregory plan to form the National Theatre Society Ltd., requesting AE to draft a constitution. Synge travels from Coole to Dublin to persuade the actors to resign from the original society of amateurs and sign professional contracts. He is elected to the Board of Directors, together with Yeats and Lady Gregory. 29 Sept., made Managing Director for six months. Plans to bring a Gaelic company from the Blasket Islands to Dublin, but by 2 Oct., when the new season opens, he is in a fever with swollen glands in his neck. Recovers sufficiently to travel with the company to Oxford, Cambridge, and London, where during the last week of Nov. all three of his plays are performed. Dec., involved in replacing actors who leave company for nationalist reasons. Contract issued to Molly Allgood as walk-on in *The Well of the Saints*. By early Dec., under the stage name of Maire O'Neill, she has taken on the role of Cathleen in *Riders to the Sea*. During the year Synge starts *The Playboy of the Western World*.

1906 Maire O'Neill replaces her older sister Sara Allgood (later to become one of Ireland's most famous actresses) as Nora Burke in *The Shadow of the Glen*. Synge courts her during rehearsals. 26 Feb., accompanies players to Wexford; his relationship with Molly is apparent to all. 26 May-9 July, travels with the company on its extensive tour of England: keeps his new relationship private from his mother by taking rooms once again in Rathgar. Becomes heavily involved with the running of the company, acting as administrator, business manager, and mediator between Yeats and the players and Willie Fay and Miss Horniman. 9 July, returns to Dublin, moves into a new house bought by his mother in Glenageary, Kingstown, to be near her daughter and son-in-law. While Mrs. Synge is in County Wicklow for the summer, Synge spends as much time as possible with Molly. Synge is now a playwright of international repute: Meyerfield's translation of *The Well of the Saints* is performed in June by Max Reinhardt's Deutsches Theater in Berlin. 7 Feb., *The Shadow of the Glen* is performed in Prague, and the Bohemian National Theatre include it in their new repertoire. Continues to write *Playboy*. 25 Aug., to aid the process Synge takes his typewriter to County Kerry: his notes and many descriptions sent to Molly became the basis of a series of articles published the following year in *The Shanachie*. 12 Sept., returns to Dublin, no further ahead with the play. Throughout autumn plagued with asthma, bronchial and stomach upsets; work continually interrupted by demands of theatre, family, and social responsibilities. 'A Translation of Irish Romance' and 'The Fair Hills of Ireland' appear in the *Manchester Guardian* (6 Mar. and 16 Nov. respectively), and 'The Vagrants of Wicklow' in the second, Nov. issue of *The Shanachie*. Nov.-Dec., proofs of *The Aran Islands* come through. His love for Molly prompts him to return to writing poetry. Suffers a severe lung infection, and Molly is obliged to visit him at home for the first time. 1-3 Dec., Synge stays with Edward in Surrey, England. Writes to his mother about his love affair with Molly Allgood. 14 Dec., returns to Dublin with *The Playboy* almost complete.

1907 Ben Iden Payne appointed to produce verse and classical plays at the Abbey; Willie Fay retains control over the dialect plays. Jan., rehearsing *Playboy*, in which Molly plays Pegeen Mike. 26 Jan., *Playboy* opens to angry response from first night audience: Lady Gregory orders cuts and telegraphs to Yeats in Aberdeen. 28 Jan., organized 'riot' causes actors to play in dumb show. 29 Jan., Yeats returns and demands police reinforcements. The newspapers report on antics of the audience in the theatre in the evening, and Yeats's performance in court during day. By Saturday the house has calmed. 4 Feb., Yeats issues a general invitation to a public debate on 'The Freedom of the Theatre'. Synge in bed with bronchitis; twice tested for tuberculosis; recurring fevers, swollen glands in neck, frequent stomach ailments heralds the as yet undiagnosed Hodgkin's disease (lymphatic sarcoma). Recovers sufficiently by 14 March to plan a summer marriage and a holiday in the West. 9 May, 'At a Wicklow Fair' published in the *Manchester Guardian*. 'On Aran Island' also published. April, with Yeats and Lady Gregory in Italy, Synge is left to manage the Abbey affairs. From 11 May, the Company tours Glasgow, Birmingham, Oxford, Cambridge, and London with *Playboy* to critical and popular acclaim. Synge convalesces with Jack Yeats in Devon. 8 June, joins the company in London, where he renews his association with John Masefield, Max Mayerfeld, and the Irish Society. Internal dissension in the Abbey company increases: Payne announces his intention to resign; Synge threatens to do so. 17 June, returns to Dublin. His doctors advise him to postpone an operation on his glands and his marriage till the autumn. 28 June, Synge and Molly go to Glencree in Wicklow instead of their planned visit to the West. He writes new poems and reworks old ones. 4 Aug., returns to Dublin. 11 Aug., company start a tour to Waterford, Cork, and Kilkenny, with *Riders* in repertoire. 14 Sept., Synge undergoes successful surgery: he is full of plans for the marriage, and works on his new play *Deirdre of the Sorrows*. 1 Dec., writes to Molly (on tour with the company in Manchester, Glasgow, and Edinburgh) that the play is ready to be read through. Troubles at the Abbey continue, bringing about Willie Fay's resignation on 13 Jan. the following year. 6 Dec., Synge develops a pain in his side.

1908 2 Feb., moves into a flat at 47 York Road, Rathmines, where he intends to live with Molly after the wedding. Feb.-March, heavily involved with Yeats in running the Abbey, where he directs performances of Lady Gregory's translations of Sudermann's *Teja* (Dutch) and Molière's *The Rogueries of Scapin. The Tinker's Wedding* published by Maunsel. Plans for the wedding go ahead despite opposition from Annie and Edward, who consider it financially impracticable. 28 April, doctors find a lump in Synge's side and he postpones wedding plans. 30 April, enters hospital: exploratory surgery reveals the tumour to be inoperable. By 24 June he recovers temporarily. 6 July, he is discharged and stays with Annie. 13 Aug., moves to Glendalough House and continues to work on *Deirdre*. Sends poems to Yeats, who intends to publish them in a limited edition for the Cuala Press. 6 Oct., leaves for Germany, arriving in Coblenz on 8 Oct., where he stays with the Von Ecken sisters. 26 Oct., Mrs. Synge dies: Synge does not return for the funeral. 7 Nov., returns to Dublin to work on, *Deirdre,* his health deteriorating: he knows he is dying.

1909 Engaged in sorting out his papers. 31 Jan., admitted to Elpis nursing home. 13 Feb., makes out his will. 14 Feb., Molly leaves for a week's visit with the company to Manchester; Synge asks Annie to write to her for him. 22 Feb., Molly returns: visits him every day until his death. 24 March, Synge dies at 5.30 a.m. 8 April, volume of *Poems and Translations* appears. 13 June 1910, *Deirdre of the Sorrows* first performed at the Abbey, directed by Molly, who also plays Deirdre. Also in 1910, Maunsel publish a four-volume edition of *The Works of J. M. Synge.*

Riders to the Sea

A tragedy in one act.
Written: 1902.
First production: Irish National Theatre Society, Molesworth
  Hall, Dublin, 25 Feb. 1904 (dir. J. M. Synge; with W. G.
  Fay as Bartley and Sara Allgood as Cathleen).
Published: in *Samhain*, Oct. 1903; *The Shadow of the Glen
  and Riders to the Sea* (London: Elkin Matthews, 1905);
  The Works of John M. Synge, Volume I (Dublin: Maunsel,
  1910); *Collected Works, Volume III: Plays, Book I*, ed.
  Ann Saddlemyer (Oxford University Press, 1968); *Riders
  to the Sea and Playboy of the Western World* (Oxford:
  Blackwell, 1969); *Complete Plays* (London: Methuen,
  1981); *Plays, Poems, and Prose* (1992).

*The scene is the kitchen of a cottage on an island off the
West of Ireland. Maurya, an old woman, has already
lost her husband, her father-in-law, and four sons to the
sea. Nine days ago another son, Michael, has been
drowned. Maurya hopes that his body will be washed
ashore and the white boards for the coffin lie ready. Her
two daughters, Cathleen and Nora, have been given
clothes from the body of a drowned man by the local
priest, but before they can determine whether the
garments belong to Michael, the youngest son, Bartley,
prepares to leave for the horse-fair across the sea in
Galway. Despite Maurya's entreaties he leaves, giving
his mother a blessing which she finds impossible to
return. Cathleen persuades Maurya to go after Bartley
to give him bread for the journey. As she leaves, the two
girls examine the bundle of clothes and Nora positively
identifies the stockings that she has knitted for Michael.
Maurya returns still holding the bread, clearly dis-
turbed. She tells the girls of the ghostly vision she has
seen while praying at the spring well: Bartley rides on
the red mare with the grey pony behind him; in the
vision, as in life, he blesses her, but as she tries to say
'God speed you', something 'choked the words' in her
throat; following on the grey pony she sees Michael*

dressed in fine clothes with new shoes on his feet. Cathleen, recognizing the significance of Maurya's premonition, begins to keen softly, saying, 'It's destroyed we are from this day.' Maurya foresees not only Bartley's death but also her own, and quietly she calls forth the dead souls of all the men in the family drowned at sea. Her daughters give her Michael's clothes as Bartley's body is carried into the kitchen, followed by men and women of the village. Bartley has been drowned also, knocked off the mare by the grey pony into the sea. He is placed on the table and Maurya, dropping Michael's clothes across his feet, sprinkles him with holy water. As the women keen softly, Maurya kneels and prays for God's mercy on her soul and all living things. She finally accepts with relief that 'the end is come'. All her menfolk are gone but so is the pain of grief at their departing. Maurya can at last look forward to the 'great rest'.

[Synge based the play on a story which he retells in Part Four of *The Aran Islands*: 'When the horses were coming down to the slip an old woman saw her son, that was drowned a while ago, riding on one of them. She didn't say what she was after seeing, and this man caught the horse, he caught his own horse first, and then he caught this one, and after that he went out and was drowned' (p. 164). The realistic detail is also from his experiences on the islands: 'Now a man has been washed ashore in Donegal with one pampooty on him, and a striped shirt with a purse in one of the pockets, and a box for tobacco' (Part Three, p. 136). And the ghostly element is informed by stories such as those referred to in Part Two, in which an old man tells of a young woman's ghost returning to her cottage to feed her child: 'She told them she was away with the fairies, and they could not keep her that night, though she was eating no food with the fairies, the way she might be able to come back to her child. Then she told them they would all be leaving that part of the country on the Oidhche Shamhna, and that there would be four or five hundred of them riding on horses, and herself would be on a grey horse, riding behind a young man. And she told them to go down to a bridge they would be crossing that night, and to wait at the head of it, and when she would be coming up she would slow the horse and they would fall over on the ground and be saved' (p. 159). The old man tells of a traveller being followed by a ghost horse: 'One night when he was coming home from the lighthouse he heard a man riding on the road behind him, and he stopped to wait for him, but nothing came. Then he heard as if there was a man trying to catch a horse on the rocks, and in a little time he went on. The noise behind him got bigger as he went along as if twenty horses, and then as if a hundred or a thousand, were galloping behind after him. When he came to the stile where he had to leave the road and got over it, something hit against him and threw him down on the rock, and a gun he had in his hand fell into the field beyond him' (p. 180).

Synge wrote the play in the summer of 1902. It is the only one of his plays set on the Aran Islands, to which he returned for the fifth and last time shortly after completing *Riders*. It is a summation of his experience of the islands, a one-act tragedy very different in structure and tone to the plays that were to follow. The play was read aloud by Lady Gregory in the presence of Synge and Yeats in London on 20 January 1903 and, according to Synge's diary, met 'with much approval'. It was read again at Yeats's on 2 February and, for the third time, a week later at Lady Gregory's, when Arthur Symons also heard it. He expressed an interest in publishing the play in *Fortnightly*, but although it was sent to Symons on 14 February, its return by *Fortnightly* was recorded in Synge's diary on 12 March. It finally appeared in the September-October issue of *Samhain* later in the year.

Riders was Synge's second play to be produced by the Irish National Theatre Society at the Molesworth Hall. Synge directed the play himself and was meticulous in his preparations, especially with regard to the stage properties. The items specifically noted in the text are of great significance and our attention is drawn to them at several points in the play. Everything has a precise function, not only as a reflection of the reality of the island people's life but also in the play's dramatic structure. George Roberts, who was in the original production, here recalls the rehearsal period.]

The rehearsals were intensely interesting. The scene, which was laid in the Aran Islands, required different treatment from any of our other peasant plays. Synge was very particular that every detail of the properties and costumes should be correct. It was found impossible to obtain material of the right shade for the Aran Islanders' petticoats (a peculiar dark crimson) until Lady Gregory discovered in Galway a man who could dye in 'madder'. Accordingly, some homespun flannel was obtained and sent to him for dyeing. The petticoats were made under Synge's directions, in a certain way, with a broad strip of calico at the top.

The pampooties were another difficulty. Synge brought in a pair he had used in the Aran Islands to show how they were made. In the islands, the raw hide of the cow or bullock is used, but the actors were squeamish at the idea of using raw hides, so we tried to get a dried skin. I went round every tanyard in Dublin, and at last succeeded in getting a calf skin that had been prepared for a farmer who had meant to make a waistcoat from it, but changed his mind when his girlfriend disapproved, and so it had been left on the tanner's hand. The members of the company, in the intervals of rehearsing, cut this up and made holes in it to make the stage pampooties.

The spinning wheel was another trouble, until Lady Gregory again came to the rescue and sent up a large wheel from Galway. Synge himself instructed the girl how to use it.

Synge was exceedingly anxious that the 'caoine' should be as close as possible to the peculiar chant that is used in the islands, and after much searching I found a Galway woman living in one of the Dublin suburbs who consented to show two of the girls how the caoine was given. She was very nervous about it, though somewhat proud that one of what she looked on as country customs should be so eagerly sought after in the city. At the same time, she was very interested in the whole affair, wanting to know what the play was about, and saying the caoine was so terrible a thing she could hardly believe people would want to put it in a play.

At first, she tried to begin in her little parlour, but she confessed after a few moments she could not do it properly there, so she brought the two girls up to a bedroom. At first it seemed no better, until she conceived the idea that I should act the corpse. She lighted the wake candles, and then she got that note full of terror of the dead. I was relieved that she did not take snuff off my belly, but apparently the candles were enough. She was a native Irish speaker, and the Irish cadences and rhythm of the words, in conjunction with the clapping of the hands and swaying of her body, made a scene very terrible and yet beautiful to look on.

George Roberts, 'The Plays of Synge',
The Irish Times, 2 Aug. 1955, p. 5

[The reviews of *Riders* were hostile in the main. *The Leader*'s reviewer called it 'the most ghastly production I have ever seen on the stage'. *The Independent* and *The Irish Times* were more moderate in their criticism but nonetheless unenthusiastic.]

Taken on its merits *Riders to the Sea* is bound to find support. Its appeal is to a cultivated taste even more than to a dramatic instinct; its studies in melancholy have hardly the poignancy of other popular works produced in the same surroundings, yet Mr. Synge, by the careful treatment of a simple theme, cannot at all be said to have been unsuccessful. . . . In the quiet backwater of the story, in the shreds and patches of character, in the tranquil life of the island Irish cottage, there is much of the old charm and delicacy, but the theme is too dreadfully doleful to please the popular taste.

Irish Daily Independent and Nation, 26 Feb. 1904

Of Mr. J. M. Synge's play, *Riders to the Sea*, it is difficult to say exactly what one thinks. The idea underlying the work is good enough; but the treatment of it is to our mind repulsive. Indeed, the play develops into something like a wake. The long exposure of the dead body before an audience may be realistic, but it certainly is not artistic. There are some things which are lifelike, and yet are quite unfit for presentation on the stage, and *Riders to the Sea* is one of them.

The Irish Times, 26 Feb. 1904

[Arthur Griffith, editor of *The United Irishman*, whose objections to *The Shadow of the Glen* had resulted in a public correspondence in the newspaper between him and W. B. Yeats, was less vehement about *Riders,* but although he appreciated 'its tragic beauty' he was equally concerned about its lack of joy.]

Mr. J. M. Synge's *Riders to the Sea*, which was presented in *Samhain* last year, was produced for the first time, and its tragic beauty powerfully affected the audience. We think, however, Mr. Synge could get his effects without the introduction of the body of a drowned man on the stage — this is a cheap trick of the Transpontine dramatists. We have seen the sea in its role of the All-Devouring and Relentless, but there is another aspect in which Irish eyes see it — the All-Purifying and All-Pitying, and we hope to see the National Theatre Society showing it in that aspect one of these days. The east wind does not always blow on the Irish soul, and there is mirth still in Erin. Up till now our stage has not been remarkable for diffusing sunshine around, and we need sunshine badly.

Arthur Griffith, *The United Irishman*, 5 Mar. 1904

[The actor George Roberts (previously quoted) recollected: 'This play . . . did not win much praise in Dublin on its first performance. Some of the audience were horrified at the sight of a corpse on stage, a few of them left the hall while the performance was going on, and the press was almost as damning as on the previous occasion of the performance of *In the Shadow of the Glen*. The adverse opinions, however, made some of us think all the more of Synge' ('The Plays of Synge', *The Irish Times*, 2 Aug. 1955, p. 5). This support from the company was reiterated by Frank Fay in a letter to Joseph Holloway shortly after the play opened.]

I am glad to say that *Riders to the Sea* despite its sadness has pleased many. I think it is a masterpiece. And after all, just at present when people shirk facing the facts and sorrow of life and are always longing for the laugh that only hardens the heart, it is good that we should put on plays of this kind. Of course I have every sympathy with the desire for laughter, if it is kindly, but there is so much laughter around that is hard and cynical and cowardly that I am not sorry we do pieces like *Riders to the Sea*. The only difficulty is that people who drop in to see us for the first time may be frightened away.

F. J. Fay, letter to J. Holloway, 1 March 1904
National Library of Ireland, Ms. No. 13,267

[On 26 March 1904 *Riders to the Sea* was performed (with *In the Shadow of the Glen*, and *The King's Threshold* by W. B. Yeats) in London. The play was greatly praised by the critics and heralded the sympathetic reception Synge was usually accorded in London in the years to come.]

The other day I came to one of the rare oases that are in the desert of our drama. For one whole afternoon my feet were on the very verdure, and there was clear cold water for my parched throat. . . . Very widely though the three plays differed from one another, from all one derived the same quality of pleasure — the pleasure in something quite simple and quite strange. There was in none of the plays any structural complexity, and yet none of them was not truly dramatic. . . . Simplicity! That was, also, the keynote of the stage setting. I have no objection to rich scenery and dresses — so long as the richness be not inappropriate or excessive. But, just for a change, how delightful to have a management which, so far from trying to dazzle us into awed calculations of its outlay, rather prides itself on its poverty. . . . As for the acting, I am not sure that so much simplicity as the players exemplified was quite artistically right. . . . For all that, I would not they had been otherwise. One could not object to them as to the ordinary amateur. They were not floundering in the effort to do something beyond their powers. With perfect simplicity, perfect dignity and composure, they were just themselves, speaking a task that they had well by heart. Just themselves; and how could such Irish selves not be irresistible? . . . Mr. Synge, being an Irishman, is content to show us the pathos of his theme. . . . 'So it is, and so it must be' is his tone. It is the tone of the mother herself . . . [who] submits not merely because it were vain to rebel. To rebel is not in her nature. She has the deep fatalism of her race; and for her, the things that actually happen, for evil as for good, are blurred through the dreams that are within her.

Max Beerbohm, *The Saturday Review*, 9 April 1904

Watch a performance of Mr. Synge's beautiful tragedy *Riders to the Sea* — so expressive of the perils of the fisherman's life, so poignant in its illustration of the phrase that men must work and women must weep — and you will perceive that mixture of resignation and protest, that dumb pathos varied with bursts of impressive passion, to be found in the Irish as in every other unspoilt kind of peasant.

The Illustrated London News, 19 Jan. 1909

[*Riders to the Sea* and *The Playboy of the Western World* are probably Synge's best known plays and the most performed. *Riders* has been translated into many languages (James Joyce, who at first disliked the play, translated it into Italian, and there are even versions in more obscure languages such as Faroese) and played throughout the world. It has also been translated into other forms, including an opera by Ralph Vaughan Williams (premiered at the Arts Theatre, Cambridge, on 22 Feb. 1938). In 1935 Gracie Fields financed an independent film version of the play with a cast of actors from the Abbey Theatre, filmed mostly in Connemara. Graham Greene's review emphasizes the pitfalls of translating the piece from one medium to another.]

There is something altogether too private about the Synge film, a touch of mutual admiration about the continual close-ups of the individual players, a self-conscious simplicity. The camera is always delayed for Synge's words, when in a true film the words are less important than the camera. I confess I am not an admirer of Synge's plays, of the idea that style is a decoration, something you can apply to your subject, instead of being an economy and exactitude. . . . But I do not think that even Synge's admirers will enjoy *Riders to the Sea*. Something has gone badly wrong with the continuity; the loss of act divisions has upset the sense of time. Though the movements of the actors between the set speeches, which are nearly always delivered in close-up, are intolerably slow, so that most of the film seems to have been spent in getting from door to fire and back again, the events outside the cottage follow quite another order of time, without interval or preparation. No sooner has one lost son been keened for than the dreary band of mourners enter to announce another death. What the film might have done, and the stage could not do so well, was to show us the manner of the deaths; it might have given us with its larger scope in space and time the sense of the poor hard lives before and after a reason for their deaths. As it is the deaths do not matter, they are merely an excuse for dirges as resonant, and as hollow, as a church bell's.

Graham Greene, *The Spectator*, 20 Dec. 1935

[Synge's haunting masterpiece did, however, provide the inspiration for Robert Flaherty's film *Man of Aran* (1934), a powerful work of poetic realism. Informed also by *The Aran Islands*, this classic film documentary eloquently shows the beauty of the islands' desolate landscape, the harshness and solitude of the islanders' life, and their indominitable spirit in their constant battle with the sea and other elements.

In 1937 Bertolt Brecht wrote *Die Gewehre der Frau Carrar* (*Senora Carrar's Rifles*), described as a modern version of Synge's *Riders to the Sea*. The play, set in an Andalusian fisherman's cottage in April 1937, was first performed in Salle Adyar, Paris, on 16 Oct. 1937, with Helene Weigel (Brecht's wife) as Carrar. A translation by Keene Wallis was published in an American magazine, *Theatre Workshop* (April-June 1938), and this version was produced by Unity Theatre in London on 13 Sept. 1938 (directed by John Fernald), and taken on tour to raise consciousness and money for Spain.

Riders to the Sea was one of the first of Synge's plays to be translated into Japanese, in 1914, other versions following in 1920, 1923, and 1938, and it has become the most read of Synge's plays in Japan. In 1938 the Japanese critic, Shotaro Oshima, records a conversation with Yeats, in which the poet said: 'I would often go for inspiration to the Japanese, who create such great beauty, especially when I was writing *Plays for Dancers*. . . . We must have a national literature. Have you seen Synge's *Riders to the Sea* performed at the Abbey Theatre? It is characteristic of our race.' . . . 'Yes', I answered, 'and I was much impressed by the rhythmical recitation of poetic words in the play. I'm sure there is nothing like that in English literature. We would have to go to the Noh theatre to find its equal.' Yeats nodded seriously and said, 'There was argument about the performance of the play, and opinion was divided especially on its production. But finally it was decided that the play should be produced in the way you have seen. There was good reason for coming to that decision. I hope you found in it the ancient, passionate Ireland. A nation or a race should remember its own heroic tradition' ('Synge in Japan', *A Century Tribute to J. M. Synge*, p. 259).

An American revival in 1957 was reviewed by Brooks Atkinson, a champion of Irish drama in the United States. He wrote two reviews for the *New York Times,* which were equally fulsome in their praise for the play and for Patricia Newell's production by the Irish Players at Theatre East.]

This native requiem recognizes a kind of tragedy that is ancient and universal, artless and plain. Synge is not merely a stylist. In this brief play he is also a poet of the human race 'in the sight of God', as his characters fearfully say at the end of nearly every sentence. . . .

Riders to the Sea has a sad glory that makes it unique. Many people regard *Riders to the Sea* as the finest one-act play in English. There will be no quibbling in this corner. The characters are valiant people. Instinctively, they have accepted the tragic irony of human existence which has to submit to the merciless caprices of nature; and they speak their thoughts with the simplicity of people who have never questioned the truth.

In the impossible working conditions of Theatre East, all the Synge plays are glowingly acted. But *Riders to the Sea* is acted particularly well in a performance that Patricia Newell has directed with strength and sensitivity.

Brooks Atkinson, *New York Times*, 10 and 17 March 1957

[In 1960 BBC Television gave an admirable account of the play, attracting the talents of a distinguished Irish designer and one of England's greatest classical actresses. There was also a good performance from a leading film star early in his acting career.]

Synge's peasant tragedy is sufficiently concentrated to need little pruning or adaptation, but Mr. George Foa's production conjured up finely the bleak, windswept coast of western Ireland, and Mr. Sean Kenny's bare, unadorned sets placed it squarely in surroundings of epic monumentality. The chief interest of the production, however, and its greatest triumph, lay in the acting. The performances of Miss Olive McFarland, Miss Jan Kenny, and Mr. Sean Connery were all beautifully in keeping, as they moved like shadows across the scene, already half-resolved, it seemed, to the grim destiny which hung over them. But the play belongs to Maurya, the old mother, and in this role Dame Sybil Thorndike gave us a superb glimpse of the grand tragic style, playing with that complete simplicity of which only the highest art is capable.

The Times, 29 Sept. 1960

[An Arabic version of *Riders to the Sea* was produced by Syrian Arab Television in July 1963. According to Ghassan Maleh: 'It could not have been presented at a better time. It was shown around 20 July, a few days after the failing of an armed attempt to take over the government, shortly after the break-up of the union between Egypt and Syria that ended with the March 1963 Baathist revolution. In July, the revolution was busy consolidating its position when other political forces made their bid for power and launched their armed attack on the radio station, army headquarters, and other key establishments in the Syrian capital. The attempted *coup d'état* crushed, curfew was imposed and tanks patrolled the streets. Meanwhile, Syrian viewers sat at home watching *Riders to the Sea* on their television sets. It was only natural for them to identify the sea that devours Maurya's sons with the just-ended political strife as well as with the forces that contended for power. The sea became a symbol of those powers that controlled man, leaving him helpless and impotent.'

Riders to the Sea was performed at the Abbey Theatre on 26 April 1971 as part of the celebration marking the centenary of Synge's birth. Acording to Hugh Hunt: 'Marie Kean played the part of the bereaved Maurya with an austere dignity drained of tears, deliberately abstaining from the sing-song that too often accompanies the final lament' (*The Abbey, Ireland's National Theatre, 1904-1979*, p. 222-3).]

The Shadow of the Glen

Play in one act.
Written: 1902.
First production: Irish National Theatre Society, Molesworth Hall, Dublin, 8 Oct. 1903 (with W. G. Fay as the Tramp and Maire Nic Shiubhlaigh as Nora).
Published: in *Samhain*, Dec.1904; *The Shadow of the Glen and Riders to the Sea* (London: Elkin Matthews, 1905); *The Works of John M. Synge, Volume I* (Dublin: Maunsel, 1910); *Collected Works, Volume III: Plays, Book I*, ed. Ann Saddlemyer, (Oxford University Press, 1968); *Complete Plays* (1981); *Plays, Poems, and Prose* (1992).

It is an old theme — that of a fine, lusty woman (Nora Burke) tied to an old wheezy man, who, to find her out, pretends to be dead. She engages herself to a timid, callow young farmer, who thinks he owns the woman. To them a tramp enters the cottage for shelter from a stormy night. She is a courageous woman, for when the tramp suggests she be afraid of him, she says, 'I'm thinking many would be afeard, but I never knew what way to be afeard of beggar or bishop, or any one of you at all.' The tramp, a natural poet, after her old husband had jumped from where he lay, supposedly dead, to denounce her, and order her out of the house, persuades the woman to come out of her loneliness and go the roads with him. . . .

In a short preface to this play Synge says that his plays hold no messages; but here, in this one, is the call of a brave heart for the fullness of life; a character ready, at last, to go through life with a steady step, and add its vigour to the energetic and everlasting song of nature. The play is alive with realism (as all of them are); but the realism is coloured gaily with imagination, and a gay, or a lovely sad song sings a merry and delightful way through each of them.

Sean O'Casey, *Blasts and Benedictions* (London: Macmillan, 1967)

[*In the Shadow of the Glen*, as it was first called, is based on a story told to Synge by Pat Durane, the old shanachie (story-teller) of Inishmaan, in 1898. Robin Skelton summarizes the story.]

The shanachie tells how, on a rainy night, while travelling from Galway to Dublin, he came across a house in which a solitary woman sat watching a man laid out on a bed as if he were dead. The woman gave the shanachie shelter and asked him to watch by the corpse while she went out to tell her friends of his death. When the woman had gone the 'corpse' sat up and told the shanachie, 'I've got a bad wife so I let on to be dead the way I'd catch her at her goings on!' The woman returned to the cottage with a young man whom she sent into the bedroom to rest. In a little while she joined the young man in the bedroom. The husband waited for a few minutes and then got out of bed and took up a stick and gave the shanachie another, and both men went into the bedroom, and when they saw the wife and her companion together, the husband 'hit the young man with the stick so that his blood leapt up and hit the gallery!'

Robin Skelton, The Writings of J. M. Synge, p. 53-4

[The play's atmosphere and depiction of character are informed by Synge's knowledge of the Wicklow area. In his essay 'The Oppression of the Hills' he writes: 'Among the cottages that are scattered through the hills of County Wicklow I have met with many people who show in a singular way the influence of a particular locality. These people live for the most part beside old roads and pathways where hardly one man passes in the day, and look out all the year on unbroken barriers of heath. At every season heavy rain falls for often a week at a time, till the thatch drips with water stained to a dull chestnut and the floor in the cottages seems to be going back to the condition of the bogs near it. The clouds break, and there is a night of terrific storm from the south-west — all the larches that survive in these places are bowed and twisted towards the point where the sun rises in June — when the winds come down through the narrow glens with the congested whirl and roar of a torrent, breaking at times for sudden moments of silence that keep up the tension of the mind. At such times the people crouch all night over a few sods of turf and the dogs howl in the lanes. . . . This peculiar climate, acting on a population that is already lonely and dwindling, has caused or increased a tendency towards nervous depression among the people, and every degree of sadness, from that of the man who is merely mournful to that of the man who has spent half his life in the madhouse, is common among these hills' (*Collected Works, Volume II: Prose*, p. 209). Here, Maire nic Shiubhlaigh, the actress who was to create the part of Nora, recalls the first time she heard the play.]

It was early in June, 1903 that Lady Gregory called us to her rooms at the Nassau Hotel and read Synge's play over to us. . . . The plot, strictly speaking, was not original, but the treatment was. It was completely different to anything we had known before; the play itself was a masterpiece of dramatic construction. It was, in fact, the first of the Irish 'realist' dramas, and the quiet young man who sat unobtrusively in the background while Lady Gregory read aloud his words, was to take his place amongst the greatest dramatists the Irish theatre produced.

Maire nic Shiubhlaigh, 'An Un-Irish Play',
J. M. Synge: Interviews and Recollections, ed. E. H. Mikhail
(London: Macmillan, 1977), p. 22

[Rehearsals were held in the Camden Hall, owned by the Fays. The cast had initial difficulty in dealing with the unfamiliar rhythms of Synge's idiosyncratic language, but he advised them to 'speak the lines for the meaning and the melody will come up'. Fay's account of rehearsals, his own contribution to and his collaboration with Synge on the production is revealing with regard to the working process and perceptive about the critics' and the public's response to the play.]

In the Shadow of the Glen was his first effort, but it showed little sign of the 'prentice hand'. It was a peasant play, but oh, how different from any of our other peasant pieces! It was the first of the modern Irish realist plays. From beginning to end there was not a syllable of sentiment. The dialect used was entirely strange to us, which was hardly surprising seeing that Synge had invented it himself. His device was the simple enough one of translating practically word for word from Gaelic. It has been imitated often since, but it was new then, and to me as producer it presented a serious problem. I was quite at home with the traditional 'stage Irish' of the 'arrah', 'begob', 'and 'bedad' school as well as the stage Irish of O'Keeffe, Boucicault, and Whitbread. . . . It was . . . disconcerting to me to encounter an Irish dialect that I could not speak 'trippingly on the tongue'.

The droll thing was that neither would Synge speak it! In time I mastered it, but he never did — perhaps partly because his years abroad had removed every trace of brogue from his speech — though he could always check it when he heard it spoken. He came to Dublin for the rehearsals — a tawny thick-set fellow with the head of a lion and a tempting moustache, and looking at least forty, though actually he was just turned thirty-two. He and I soon got together and experimented with the dialogue until, after much hard practice, I got at how the speeches were built up, and would say any of the lines exactly in the way he wanted. They had what I call a balance of their own, and went with a kind of lilt: 'she had the lightest hand . . . at making a cake . . . or milking a cow . . . that wouldn't be aisy!' Once I had found out the proper 'time' I never had any difficulty with the dialect in any of his other plays.

Synge always finished a play in his mind to the last detail before he started writing it down, and once it was on paper he could not alter it. I remember asking him once if he did not think that a certain speech might be improved. He replied, I quite agree, but these were the words he used and I only set them down. He told me that as the play came into being in his imagination the characters took on a life of their own and said and did things without consulting him at all. It is a fact that you cannot cut a line in any of his plays without damaging the whole structure. His power of visualization was perfect. I would work out a scale plan of the stage and furniture, and he would say, 'That is just the way I saw the room as I was writing the play.' It was very lucky that there seemed to be a sort of pre-established harmony between my mind and his, for I always wanted to produce his plays as nearly as possible as he saw them. If I asked him, 'Was Dan standing where he is on the right, behind the table, when he said these lines,' he would say, 'No, he was on the right-hand side of the table with his hand on it.' He was a great joy to work with, for he had a keen sense of humour and patience, and above all he knew what he wanted, and when he got it said so — which is a virtue very rare in dramatic authors.

The treatment meted out to Synge during his lifetime might well have stirred the rest of the world to wonder if Irishmen really had any sense of humour. A possible explanation of this peculiar obtuseness, this complete inability to appreciate satire except when it is directed at other nations, is that, until our movement forced one upon them, the Gaels never had a theatre of their own and therefore little understanding of the functions and values of the stage. They had not the needful sophistication to accept a play as a play and leave it at that. Instead of being convulsed with laughter at the stark comedy of *In the Shadow of the Glen* they were convulsed with what Oscar Wilde calls 'the rage of Caliban at seeing his own face in the glass'.

W. G. Fay '*In the Shadow of the Glen*',
J. M. Synge: Interviews and Recollections, ed. E.H. Mikhail
(London: Macmillan, 1977), p. 26-8

[The hostility towards the play started from within the company during rehearsals. Dudley Digges and Maire Quinn alleged that the play ridiculed Irish womanhood. Synge refused to remove or change the parts of the text to which they objected and, in protest, they resigned from the Irish National Theatre Society. Maud Gonne and Douglas Hyde also resigned in support. On the day of the first performance someone (possibly Dudley Digges) leaked the plot to the *Irish Independent*, the most powerful and conservative newspaper in circulation. The paper asserted that 'Synge knows more about the boulevards of Paris than the fishing folk of the Aran Islands' and urged the Irish National Theatre Society to reject 'this perversion of their aims'.

The play was performed between two of Yeats's plays, *The King's Threshold* and *Cathleen Ni Houlihan*. The audience remained respectful at the end of the evening largely due to a characteristically stern speech delivered to them from the stage by Yeats. The reviews however were varied.]

This production which has led to a secession, or schism, in the Society, was received with mingled cheers and hisses. Personally, we think that the morality which would be injured by witnessing it must have been so excessively weak-kneed to start with as to be quite unworthy of consideration. But to speak candidly, while admitting the cleverness of the dialect and the excellent acting of Nora and the tramp (Mr. W. G. Fay), we found it exceedingly distasteful. [The plot] seems to us an extraordinary choice of subject for a society that claims to have a higher and purer standard than ordinarily accepted in things dramatic.

The Irish Times, 9 Oct. 1903

Taken by itself, the play was most agreeable fooling. It has qualities which mark it out as quite apart from, and in some sense beyond, the usual type of production at the National Theatre. There is a convincing ring of truth, not necessarily in the sense that the characters represented are typical of Irish life; but trust, as meaning that the actions and characters are quite possible in real life, consequently in Irish life.

The Daily Express, 9 Oct 1903

While Ireland stood in the dock the fierce-tempered part of the nation which moulded Swift's mind remained apart, too scornful to plead, tongue-tied by pride.

But Ireland is no longer in the dock. She has shipped out of all the toils of her oppressors. She is sufficient to herself. Let her therefore put her house in order in accordance with her own judgement and conscience; let her begin the work of self examination and self-accusation.

These few remarks are by way of salutation to Mr. Synge's play now being produced at the Irish National Theatre. Putting aside the pretty and caring nothing for the idyllics, Mr Synge has attacked our Irish institution, the loveless marriage.

With a sort of joy expressed in the lightest and most copious comedy its author shows us a young girl having every instinct of womanhood uprooted by marriage with a man crabbed from age and avarice. The play is indescribable — for the man who laughs there is fun 'fast and furious'; to the man who feels, every incident (and every incident is a surprise) conveys a deep mournfulness. All are relieved when at the end of the scene the young wife goes away with a young tramp who tempts her by his life on the open highway and under the open sky — better be a young tramp's drudge, better be a target for everyone's scorn, better anything than the foulness of such a marriage. . . .

I do not know whether Mr. Synge is as great as Shakespeare, but he has begun well. And I cannot conceive any event more important in Irish history for some time to come, than a few more plays by him.

I am among those Irish people who think we should take no criticism from our enemies, Briton or West-Briton. But Mr. Synge has the true Irish heart — he lives in Aran, speaks Irish, and knows the people. He is, besides, a man of insight and sincerity, that is to say, a man of genius. Such men are the salt of Ireland.

John Butler Yeats, *The United Irishman*, 10 Oct. 1903

The Irish National Theatre Society was ill-advised when it decided to give its imprimatur to such a play as *In a Wicklow Glen* [sic]. The play has an Irish name, but it is no more Irish than the *Decameron*. It is a staging of a corrupt version of the old-world libel on womankind — the 'Widow of Ephesus', which was made current in Ireland by the hedge-schoolmaster. Last week Mr. J. B. Yeats wrote in our columns about this play: 'I do not know whether Mr. Synge is as great as Shakespeare.' Now that we have seen Mr. Synge's play, we are no longer in any doubt on the point. To take the Widow of Ephesus and rechristen her Mrs. Burke, and relabel Ephesus Wicklow, is not a brilliant thing. Any one of us possessed of no modicum of Shakespeare's genius might do it, and, provided we had assimilated as much of the decadent cynicism that passes current in the Latin Quarter and the London salon for wit, produce a like play. There is no reason, indeed now that Mr. Synge has turned a Greek lady into an Irish peasant woman and Ephesus into Wicklow, why he should not transform Alibech, by a wave of his magic pen, into a Dublin girl and place the hermit's cave in the Fairy Glen — why he should not evolve us one hundred Irish plays out of the stories Boccaccio gave the Florentines. Mr. Synge, indeed, we believe, could give us good plays, even great plays, if he studied the people of whom he writes. Yet although Mr. Synge speaks Irish and resides for a period each year in Aran, this play of his shows him to be as utterly a stranger to the Irish character as any Englishman who has yet dissected us for the enlightenment of his countrymen. His Wicklow tramp who addresses an Irish peasant woman as 'the lady of the house', and his Wicklow farmer's wife who addresses the man who has craved her hospitality as 'stranger', never existed in the flesh in Wicklow nor in any of the thirty-two counties. . . . Synge's mode of attack is not to be commended. . . .

Man and woman in rural Ireland, according to Mr. Synge, marry lacking love, and, as a consequence, the woman proves unfaithful. Mr. Synge never found that in Irish life. Men and women in Ireland marry lacking love, and live mostly in a dull level of amity. Sometimes they do not — sometimes the woman lives in bitterness — sometimes she dies of a broken heart — but she does not go away with the Tramp.

Arthur Griffith, 'All Ireland', *The United Irishman*, 17 Oct. 1903

[James Connolly (one of the leaders of the 1916 uprising) added his voice to the play's detractors. He maintained that the theatre should support 'the forces of virile nationalism in their fight against the widespread spirit of decadence, instead of undermining them.' Maud Gonne also felt obliged to speak out.]

A National Theatre, like all other branches of national literature, must have its root deep down in the centre of national life. In Ireland it must draw its vitality from that hidden spring from which the seven fountains of Gaelic inspiration flow, where the red nuts of knowledge are ever falling, otherwise its branches will not have the strength to blossom under the blighting wind of foreign civilization and thought which has blown so long over Ireland.

Maud Gonne, 'A National Theatre',
The United Irishman, 24 Oct. 1903, p. 2-3

[Yeats engaged in a spirited defence of Synge's play in the columns of *The United Irishman*. On 24 October his essay appeared entitled 'The Irish National Theatre and Three Sorts of Ignorance', in which he argued for the freedom of the imagination. It would seem that Connolly agreed with him in part but advocated a theatre to restore 'our proper national pride'. Maud Gonne, who favoured some of Yeats's work, commented: 'Mr. Yeats asks for freedom for the theatre, freedom even from patriotic captivity. I would ask for freedom for it from one thing more deadly than all else — freedom from the insidious and destructive tyranny of foreign influence.'

Synge refused to comment, except to say in a letter to his friend, Stephen MacKenna: 'On the French stage you get sex without the balancing elements. On the Irish stage you get the other elements without the sex. The people were so surprised they saw sex only.' He did, however, respond two years later when Arthur Griffith revived the discussion about the source of the play. Synge wrote a letter to *The United Irishman* which Griffith published on 1 Feb. 1905: 'Sir, I beg to enclose the story of an unfaithful wife which was told me by an old man on the middle island of Aran in 1898, and which I have since used in a modified form in *The Shadow of the Glen*. It differs essentially from any version of the story of the Widow of Ephesus with which I am acquainted. As you will see, it was told to me in the first person, as not infrequently happens in folktales of this class. Yours etc., J. M. Synge.' Griffiths printed the letter but neglected to include the story. The original version of this story is in *Collected Works, Volume III: Plays, Book I*, p. 254-5, and in its more polished form in *The Aran Islands*, Part 1, (*Collected Works, Volume II: Prose*, p. 70-2).

On 26 March 1904 *In the Shadow of the Glen* was performed at the Royalty Theatre in London with *Riders to the Sea* and Yeats's *The King's Threshold*. Synge's other play captured the imagination of the critics and little was said about this one. However, in his review of a revival in 1909 (again with *Riders*), during the Abbey Company's visit to the Court Theatre in June 1909, Max Beerbohm acknowledged the quality of the piece.]

J. M. Synge [is] that most remarkable of the dramatists who responded to the Irish literary movement. *In the Shadow of the Glen* is, in the bare outline of it, a kind of farce. . . . Absurd enough the story sounds. . . . But Synge made of it a thing not merely of rich humour, but of deep poetic quality, breathing into it a sense of lonely and humble lives, and (through the persons of the wife and the tramp) a true philosophy.

Max Beerbohm, *The Saturday Review*, 12 June 1909

[The realism demanded by Synge in the production's scenic elements — Dan Burke's cottage was carefully copied from life — and his and Fay's views on the speaking of poetic language did much to establish the style of acting and production which became known as 'the Abbey method'. Before their first extensive tour in 1906 a brochure was produced which explained the theory behind the method: 'The Folk Play needs a special kind of acting, and the Company selected to interpret the programme are all familiar with the ways of the Irish peasantry, and in their acting take care to keep close to the actual movements and gestures of the people. Therefore costumes and their properties are not the haphazard collection from the theatre store, but thoroughly appropriate and accurate, while the scenes in which they play are actual replicas of some carefully chosen original; forasmuch as these plays are portions of Irish life, so are they put upon the stage with a care and accuracy of detail that has hardly been attempted before' *Collected Works, Volume III: Plays, Book I*, p. xix).

Austin Harrison described the productions at the Court as 'a revelation . . . the best things literary and histrionic at this season in London'. He also analyzed in some detail the effects of 'the Abbey method', particularly with regard to the actors' speech.]

English is not considered a musical language, but the speech of these Irish players is as musical as Italian or Russian. This alone makes a visit to the Court a keen and artistic pleasure. Of course, they have been very carefully trained, taught the sense of words, the use of stress and modulation, the beauty of form — and the result is a flow of speech which ripples like the splashing of laughing waters. The Irish voice is naturally round, full, melodious, lulling. I have never heard the English language sound so graceful and musical before. The sibilant characteristics of the tongue are unnoticeable. Nothing jars, neither word nor stage action. And the language itself is singularly beautiful. As in Spanish, one notices in Mr. Synge's plays a sense of assonance, a fine feeling for rhythm, a rounding off of phrases, a poetic form which, while they never intrude, never strike upon the ear as sought for or 'vonia', are all the more delightful for the quiet distinction of manners and diction attained by the players. At first it is almost like listening to a foreign tongue. Yet you lose all sense of artifice and of the stage. None of them addresses the footlights. No one poses or postures. The thing is a whole.

Austin Harrison, *The Observer*, 13 June 1909

[*The Shadow of the Glen* has been translated into many languages since these early performances. Paul Karel Musek translated it into Czech in 1905 with a subsequent production at the Inchover Theatre in Prague in February 1906. There is even a Korean version, which received its first performance in April 1925 at the Kwang-Mu-Duc Theatre in Seoul. However, the play has had few major revivals. In 1954 BBC Television broadcast *The Shadow of the Glen* and, although it was not ideally suited to the medium, something of the play's originality was conveyed.]

J. M. Synge's early one-act play may be short and farcical, but its implications are most consciously placed, copious, and profound.

Last night's television performance conveyed well the farce of the 'dead' man jumping up in bed to surprise his wife and her lover, but the production did not quite succeed in the more difficult task of suggesting the rich overtones with which the playwright subtly invested this laughable situation. Nora Burke goes off at the finish with a passing stranger; it is the lonesome glen which really drives her away, not her senile husband or her weak lover. Just as the sea is the protagonist in Synge's more famous one-act piece, so here the reality of the isolated and immemorial setting is the deepest reality of the play; and here, of course, television is at a great disadvantage. How at present, for instance, is a cottage 'where there aren't two living souls would see the light you have shining' to be shown to us? Yet only in this atmosphere do the resounding Irish phrases tell.

But if their background did not come through, the peasant characters themselves did most considerably. The humorous contrast between the wizened, thirsty old age and passionately mercenary youth was spiritedly sketched by Mr. Stephen Boyd and Mr. Eric Ferguson; Miss Siobhán McKenna played the fickle wife with dignity and restraint, and Mr. Liam Gaffney struck a fine mellow chord as the tramp who invites the lady of the house to leave the misty glen and seek with him a grand morning.

The Times, 12 August 1954

[*The Shadow of the Glen* was one of the three plays chosen to mark the Golden Jubilee of the Abbey, which was celebrated in December 1954. Two hundred guests, including the President, the Taoiseach, and other distinguished guests watched Synge's play performed with Yeats's *On Baile's Strand* and Lady Gregory's *Spreading the News*. In 1968 the Abbey presented the play, together with O'Casey's *The Shadow of a Gunman*, at the Teatro della Pergola, Florence, for the city's annual festival in April. In 1982, the BBC broadcast Bernard Steven's one-act opera based on the play, with a libretto attributed to Synge, and in the same year the Druid Theatre Company from Galway chose *The Shadow of the Glen* as a late-night show for the Edinburgh Festival.]

Druid Theatre have developed from small beginnings into a company with an impressive command of their art. Their rendering of Synge's *Shadow of the Glen* is a perfect and pleasing miniature, a fine example of small-scale, acutely observed drama. The play, Synge's first, is very short and might appear at first sight to possess little substance, but its simplicity is deceptive, fired as it is by the author's inimitable, musical language — romantic evocations of the 'back hills' of Wicklow combined with broad, peasant comedy.

The story of a young woman trapped in a lonely and loveless marriage with an old man, *Shadow of the Glen* draws fine performances from all four members of the cast, but it is Marie Mullen as Nora Burke, the young wife, who shines. It is good, above all, to hear a strong Irish cast doing justice to Synge's language and managing to combine comic acting with lyricism and tragedy.

Ian Bell, *The Scotsman*, 2 Sept. 1982

The Tinker's Wedding

A comedy in two acts.
Written: 1902-04.

First production: Afternoon Theatre Company, His Majesty's Th.,
    London, 11 Nov. 1909.
Published: Dublin: Maunsel, 1908; *The Works of John M. Synge,
    Volume I* (Dublin: Maunsel, 1910); *Collected Works, Volume IV:
    Plays, Book 2*, ed. Ann Saddlemyer (Oxford University Press, 1968);
    The Complete Plays (1981); *Plays, Poems, and Prose* (1992).

*Sarah Casey wishes to marry Michael Byrne, with whom she has
been living for many years and by whom she has borne many
children, in order to be recognized as a respectable woman. The
Priest will only marry the couple if he can have a tin can, the
making of which is the tinker's main occupation. Mary Byrne,
Michael's mother, unwittingly prevents the marriage by selling
the tin can for porter, replacing it with empty beer bottles. When
the Priest discovers the trick he refuses to marry the couple and
threatens them with the police. They tie him up in a sack and
make their escape, destined to remain unmarried.*

[Synge started work on *The Tinker's Wedding* in 1902 at the same time
as he was writing *Riders to the Sea* and *The Shadow of the Glen*. It is the
third of his shanachie plays. The story upon which the plot is based, and
which he included in his essay 'At a Wicklow Fair', was told to him by a
shepherd in Wicklow: 'That man is a great villain. . . . One time he and
his woman went up to a priest in the hills and asked him would he wed
them for half a sovereign, I think it was. The priest said it was a poor
price, but he'd wed them surely if they'd make him a tin can along with
it. "I will, faith," said the tinker, "and I'll come back when it's done."
They went off then, and in three weeks they came back, and they asked
the priest a second time would he wed them. "Have you the tin can?"
said the priest. "We have not", said the tinker, "we had it made at the fall
of night, but the ass gave it a kick this morning, the way it isn't fit for
you at all." "Go on now", says the priest, "It's a pair of rogues and
schemers you are, and I won't wed you at all." They went off then, and
they were never married to this day' (*Collected Works, Volume II:
Prose*, p. 228-9).

The Irish National Theatre Society were wary about producing the
new play, given the reception received by *The Shadow of the Glen* and
Riders. By 1904 Synge had completed a two-act version of the play, and
on 9 September 1905 Yeats wrote that 'we may find it too dangerous for
the theatre at present.' In a letter to Max Meyerfeld (his German
translator) in 1906, Synge described it as 'a little play written before *The
Well of the Saints* but never played here because it is thought too

immoral and anticlerical.' When Meyerfeld eventually received the manuscript he considered it 'too undramatic and too Irish' for Germany. Yeats's caution proved to be well founded: here, Joseph Holloway describes the response when the play was eventually published by Maunsel in Dublin in 1908.]

The poster THE WRITER OF THE PLAYBOY OF THE WESTERN WORLD INSULTS THE PRIESTHOOD caught my attention as I walked downtown in the afternoon, and I was determined to possess a copy of the poster. Failing to get one in the news shop, I called at the office and was successful in securing one. The article was headed THE PLAYBOY OF THE WESTERN WORLD, FAMOUS PLAY OUTDONE IN NEW PIECE, A VULGAR ATROCITY, GROSS LIBEL ON THE PRIESTHOOD OF IRELAND. The writer starts with — 'Not content with his achievement in the direction of *The Playboy of the Western World,* Mr. J. M. Synge has perpetrated a still greater atrocity in the new play *The Tinker's Wedding.* The thing is an abominable libel upon the Irish priesthood. No such travesty has even been penned before. And it is safe to say that if the precious production is ever presented on an Irish stage the consequence will put the exciting scenes witnessed at the performance of *The Playboy of the Western World* completely in the shade.' The writer goes on to describe the plot and winds up, 'This may be '"art": it may be "comedy" in Mr. Synge's opinion. But it is safe to say once more that if this scurrilous "comedy" is ever played before an Irish house, the actors who play it and the people who sanction its production will be taught a lesson that will make them sadder, if wiser, men.'

Joseph Holloway, *Impressions of a Dublin Playgoer,* 26 Jan. 1908

[On 7 August 1907, Synge wrote to Frank Sidgwick (publisher of Yeats's work in England), 'I have a short play *The Tinker's Wedding* which has never been produced and I will be very glad to show it to Mr. Granville Barker. . . . We have never acted it here as it would have made a greater disturbance, if possible, than the *Playboy' (Collected Plays, Volume IV: Plays, Book 2,* p. xv). Granville Barker, the playwright and critic who had been running the Court Theatre, where many of Shaw's early plays were produced, replied to Synge on 18 September 1907: 'Three things about *The Tinker's Wedding.* I want my partner (J. E. Vedrenne) to see it. I want us to think whether we can really get the Irish atmosphere, without which it would be a cruelty to you to play it. And I want to see what sort of bill we could fit it into. If this delay is intolerable to you, please let me know.' And later on 2 December 1907: 'I have kept your play a disgraceful time. . . . I am very interested in *The Tinker's Wedding*; whether Redford [of the Lord Chamberlain's office] would pass it or not I don't know. I am unaware of his views on the Irish question, or whether he has any. Probably he regards Ireland as a benighted place, since it is not in his moral keeping. But one of my dificulties is that I doubt if we could do it here; I doubt if our actors could capture it' *(Collected Works*, p. xv-xvi). Barker's fears were realized when *The Tinker's Wedding* received its premiere production in London on 11 November 1910, over a year after Synge's death. Yeats walked out after the first act, and *The Times* reviewer described it as 'less a play than a picture of Irish life in its more squalid aspects. . . . The climax of the piece, in which the priest, in full canonicals, is gagged and put into a sack, seems a little far-fetched to English audiences, but the whole is a vivid and effective little work.']

Described as a comedy in two acts, this posthumous piece proved to have no dramatic significance whatsoever, but to be merely a study of sordid peasant life, which was quite uninteresting, and of dialect which was sometimes so good as to be almost incomprehensible. . . . Miss Mona Limerick gave a mournfully pretty telling cadence to the speeches of a young tinker-woman anxious to get a huckstering priest to marry her at a reduced fee, while Miss Clare Greet was repulsively life-like as the drunken mother of the prospective bridegroom. But *The Tinker's Wedding* was a dismal, whining business, which but for the nationality of its perpetrator would probably have been resented as another injustice to Ireland.

The Observer, 14 Nov. 1910

Of course we get . . . that haunting Irish cadence and those poetical flights of fancy which have always been characteristics of Mr. Synge's dialogue. But there is no movement 'or dramatic significance in the piece, and the best that can be said for it is that is is a study of the seamier side of Irish peasant life, in which a travelling tinker, his unmarried mate, his drunken and repulsive old mother, and a priest who haggles like a chapman over his fees for performing a wedding are presented realistically enough, but are not made to react upon one another in an interesting manner. They come before us amid rather sordid surroundings; they use a dialect that to English ears is only half intelligible, and when the three tramps disappear from the scene after playing a scurvy trick on the priest, we are glad to bid the whole set goodbye.

E. M., *Illustrated London News*, 20 Nov. 1910

[Since its inauspicious premiere and despite Meyerfeld's reservations about its translatability, *The Tinker's Wedding* has been produced all over the world. It was translated into Japanese in 1923, with a new version following in 1939. Shotaro Oshima claims that the mood of

Synge's plays is very much like that of a Kyogen or a farce of Japan: 'Words in Synge's plays are, like those in Kyogen, realistic and full of native directness, musical and at the same time rich in expression. The form is perfectly suited to being played on the stage in Anglo-Irish' ('Synge in Japan', *A Centenary Tribute to J. M. Synge*, p. 260). In relation to a New York production of 1957, Walter Kerr described the play as 'a rural saturnalia' *(New York Herald Tribune*, 7 March 1957), while Brooks Atkinson observed that Synge portrayed the peasant not as a romantic, but 'a sharp cunning creature of ignorance and craft who nevertheless speaks a glorious prose full of instinctive supplication to God' *(New York Times*, 7 March 1957). When Kenneth Tynan reviewed a production mounted (with *The Shadow of the Glen* and Brendan Behan's *The Big House*) as part of a two-month festival of Irish Comedy at the Theatre Royal, Stratford, East London in July 1963, he remarked that what softened Synge's 'glorious prose' was 'his determination, in all contexts to be lyrical', and his 'inability to resist a pretty simile and his insistence on writing in what, to him, was always an alien dialect' *(The Observer*, 4 August 1963). According to *The Times* reviewer, this was a 'perfunctory production', but in October of the same year the Pike Theatre, founded in Dublin ten years earlier, presented the play at the Dublin Theatre Festival with superior results.]

At the Pike Theatre one could see what roots the Irish peasant has, with Synge's *The Tinker's Wedding* in full tongue. This is what Fluther would call 'a "darling" play', a superb two-acter with sparkling dialogue. A newcomer, Angela Nolan, gave a striking performance as Sarah Casey, mingling the tinker whine effectively with vivid poetic speech, as well as displaying bold dramatic presence.

The Times, 9 October 1963

[Sean Cotter's production of the play in 1971, celebrating the centenary of Synge's birth, marked the first appearance of *The Tinker's Wedding* on the Abbey stage. Synge's own views on the comedy are recorded in the Preface to *The Tinker's Wedding*, which he completed on 2 December 1907.]

The drama is made serious — in the French sense of the word — not by the degree in which it is taken up with problems that are serious in themselves, but by the degree in which it gives the nourishment, not very easy to define, on which our imaginations live. We should not go to the theatre as we go to the chemist's, or a dram-shop, but as we go to a dinner, where the food we need is taken with pleasure and excitement. This was nearly always so in Spain and England and France when the drama was at its richest — the infancy and decay of the drama tend to be didactic — but in these days the playhouse is too often stocked with the dregs of many seedy problems, or with the absinthe or vermouth of the last musical comedy.

The drama, like the symphony, does not teach or prove anything . . . — look at Ibsen and the Germans — but the best plays of Ben Jonson and Molière can no more go out of fashion than the blackberries on the hedges.

Of the things which nourish the imagination, humour is one of the most needful, and it is dangerous to limit it or destroy it. Baudelaire calls laughter the greatest sign of the Satanic element in man; and where a country loses its humour, as some towns in Ireland are doing, there will be morbidity of mind, as Baudelaire's mind was morbid.

In the greater part of Ireland, however, the whole people, from the tinkers to the clergy, have still a life, and view of life, that are rich and genial and humorous. I do not think that these country people, who have so much humour themselves, will mind being laughed at without malice, as the people in every country have been laughed at in their own comedies.

Synge, *Collected Works, Volume IV: Plays, Book 2*, p. 3

The Well of the Saints

Play in three acts.
Written: 1903-04, and revised 1908.
First production: Irish National Theatre Society, Abbey Theatre, Dublin, 4 Feb. 1905 (with W. G. Fay as Martin Doul, Sara Allgood as Molly Byrne, and Maire Nic Shiubhlaigh as the Bride).
Published: London: A. H. Bullen, 1905; *The Works of John M. Synge, Volume I* (Dublin: Maunsel, 1910); *Collected Works, Volume III: Plays, Book I*, ed. Ann Saddlemyer (Oxford University Press, 1968); *Complete Plays* (1981); *Plays, Poems, and Prose* (1992).

Two blind married beggars, Martin and Mary Doul ('doul' is gaelic for 'blind') are convinced of their own beauty and attraction by the apparently friendly deception perpetrated and continued by their friends and acquaintances. A wandering saint, who carries with him holy water from a secret well, heals the two beggars of their affliction. The couple discover that they are in fact ugly, as is the apparently civilized world around them. Martin leaves his wife and pays court to the beautiful Molly

*Byrne, who at first encourages him but later shames him as his
blindness returns. In their renewed state of darkness, Mary and
Martin discover one another again and consciously choose to
maintain the illusion of their former life.*

[In his notebooks, Synge gives an account of his discovery of a holy
well on his first visit to Aran in May 1889. This later appeared in *The
Aran Islands*.]

At the church of St. Carolan which I have visited with my guide there is
a holy well remarkable for many cures. While we loitered in the
neighbourhood an old man came to us from a near cottage and told us
how it became famous. A woman of Sligo had one son who was blind.
She dreaming of a well that held water potent to cure so she took boat
with her son following the course of her dream and reached Aran. She
came to the house of my informant's father and told what had brought
[her] but when those around offered to lead her to the well nearby she
declined all aid saying she saw still the way clear before [her]. She led
her son from the [house] and going a little up the hill stopped at the well.
Then kneeling with the blind child beside her she prayed [to] God and
bathed his eyes. In a moment his face gleamed with joy as he said, 'Oh
Mother look at the beautiful flowers.' Twice since the same story has
been told to me with unimportant variations yet ending always with the
glad dramatic cry of the young child.

Synge, *Collected Works, Volume III*, p. 263-4

[In the spring of 1895 and winter of 1896-97 Synge attended courses
given at the Sorbonne by Professor Petit de Julleville, the author of
Histoire du Théâtre en France au Moyen-âge. On 3 October 1903 he
noted sections of Chapters II and III of the volume *La Comédie et les
Moeurs au Moyen-âge* (1886). These include a description of Andrieu
de la Vigne's *Moralité de l'Aveugle et du Boiteux* (1456), 'an early
French farce'. Synge told Padraic Colum that this piece had inspired *The
Well of the Saints*. Greene and Stephens (*J. M. Synge, 1871-1909*)
summarize the plot: 'A blind man agrees to carry a crippled man on his
back so that each can compensate for the other. The arrangement is
completely successful until they are both cured by passing a procession
in which the remains of St. Martin are displayed. The blind man is
delighted, but the cripple curses the saint for destroying an easy life on
the back of his companion' (p. 140).

Synge began work on the play in 1903, completing it the following
year. He continued to work on it even after the first production in 1905.
It was revived in 1908, designed by Charles Ricketts, for which
production Synge rewrote Act Three. Robin Skelton believes that these

amendments after production and publication are due to Synge's awareness that 'in this play of all plays exactitude of speech was important.']

The reason for this is easy to see. In *The Well of the Saints* the two central characters build up their sense of identity by means of conversation and daydream rather than by action. We do not have an object at the centre of the play, as we have the clothes at the centre of *Riders to the Sea* and the tin can at the centre of *The Tinker's Wedding*. We do not have the dramatic suspense and mystery of *The Shadow of the Glen*. The play, indeed, opens with two beggars entering, sitting down, and talking. During the greater part of the first act there is little movement. It was the more important for Synge, therefore, to establish exactly the finer details. . . . In *The Tinker's Wedding* there are . . . extremely detailed stage directions, and many of them are interpretive. *The Well of the Saints,* however, exceeds them all in the quantity and detailed nature of its directions. This is not only because the play frequently lacks physical movement, but also because it is essentially a psychological drama, in which the alterations of attitude and mood provide the dramatic rhythm, rather than the events which stimulate these movements.

Robin Skelton, *The Writings of J. M. Synge*, p. 92-3

[The play went into rehearsal in the summer of 1904, supervised by William Fay. Yeats saw a rehearsal in August and sent Synge the letter which follows.]

I saw your play rehearsed in Dublin, or rather I saw the first act several times. Of course it was imaginative and original from the very first, but at first I was inclined to think that it would lack climax, gradual and growing interest. Then I forced myself to attend to the picture of the eye, the bell in the girl's hand, the cloak, the withered faces of the old people, and I saw that these things made all the difference. It will be very curious, beautiful and exciting.

One or two criticisms occurred to me. There is a place where you make the saint say that some one of the characters has a low voice or should have a low voice and that this is a good thing in women. This suggests that he has been reading *King Lear*, where Cordelia's voice is described as low, 'an excellent thing in woman'. I think this is a wrong association in the mind. I do not object to another passage about the spells of smirhs and women which suggests that he has been reading St. Patrick's hymn. He might naturally have done so. The point is not however very important. But I do think it of some importance that you should cross out a number of the Almighty Gods. I do not object to them on the ground that they are likely to shock people but because the phrase occurs so often that it may weary and irritate the ear. I remember the disastrous effect of the repetition of the word beauty in the last act of Edward Martyn's *Maeve*. I daresay that people do repeat the word very often, but unhappily the stage has its laws which are not those of life. Fay told me that you gave him leave to cross out what he will, but though he is very anxious to reduce the number of the God Almightys, he does not like to do it of himself. . . .

W. B. Yeats, in Synge, *Collected Works, Volume III*, p. xxi-xxii

[Synge, meticulous as ever, tried to explain the play to the company, as is evidenced by his notes to Fay.]

If it is possible — Timmy, Molly should be got to show that in all their relations with Martin and Mary — friendly as they are — they feel their own superiority — for this reason Timmy's slapping Martin on back etc is better left out.

Timmy's key-note is that he's always telling queer things and the lot of them nothing at all — thus he runs up before all the others to tell the news — when the saint appears he comes forward with a long speech about Martin [and Mary] and so on — he is a good-natured naive busy-body with a hot temper — i.e. that is how I felt him, but of course it is quite possible that in the necessarily slight sketch of him this did not come out strongly enough to tell on stage. . . .

A marked difference of voice and bearing should be felt when the saint goes into church and the people are left to themselves.

Getting up in the morning and eating her food etc. pianissimo and slow from that crescendo up to where he goes blind and stay up till he gets near end of curse when it dies off a little the feeling having become so intense that it cannot be spoken.

Synge, *Collected Works, Volume II*, p. xxiii

[And in a letter to Fay it is clear that he had no intention of changing the text in response to public opinion.]

I have just come home from our long day in the country and found your letter waiting for me. Miss G[arvey] mentioned the matter of the speech about priest to me directly but I had not time to go into matter fully with her and see what she meant. In your letter you quote your objector as saying '*these things are not true*'. What put the simile into my head was a scene I saw not long ago in Galway when I saw a young man behaving most indecently to a girl on the roadside while two priests sat near by on a seat looking out to sea and pretending not to see what was going on. The girl, of course, was perfectly well able to take care of herself and stoned the unfortunate man half a mile into Galway. The way the two priests sat stolidly looking out to sea with this screaming row going on at their elbows tickled my fancy and seemed to me rather typical of many attitudes of the Irish church party. Further though it is true — I am sorry to say — that priests do beat their *parishioners,* the man in question — in my play — may have been a tinker, stranger, sailor, cattle-drover — God knows what — types with which no priest would dream of interfering. Tell Miss G. — or whoever it may be — that what I write of Irish country life I know to be true and I most emphatically will not change a syllable of it because A, B or C may think they know better than I do. The other speech you refer to is not fresh in my mind, we can discuss it when we meet. You understand my position: I am quite ready to avoid hurting people's feeling needlessly, but I will not falsify what I believe to be true for anybody. If one began that where would one end? I would rather drop playwriting altogether.

I told Miss G. today, on the spur of the moment, that the said man in the side ditch was a Protestant and that if the priest had touched him he would have got six months with hard labour for common assault — perhaps as good an answer as any. She seems to have thought that I was sneering at the priest for not doing his obvious duty — an idea which of course never entered my head.

Synge, *Collected Works, Volume III,* p. xxiii-xxiv

[In later years Fay recalled his experience of working on the play both as director and actor.]

The Well of the Saints [is] in my opinion his best play. He gave himself a large enough canvas on which to paint the picture in his mind. He had felt what all writers of one-act plays must feel sooner or later, that the concentration demanded by a short play allows one to give only the headings and suggestions of what ought to be full scenes, if truthfully developed. . . .

When one is producing a difficult play like this it is not easy to remain objective, to see it from the point of view the audience will take on the first night. It is only after years of experience with all kinds of plays and all kinds of audiences that one acquires the working knowledge of crowd psychology that enables one to tell, while a play is still in rehearsal, whether it is likely to offend or not. That is the most one can do. I never could get either Yeats or Synge to understand that if you write plays to be acted, not read by the fireside, there are certain rules that you cannot break without destroying the sympathy between the stage and auditorium. The rules I refer to are not technical but psychological. For example, as *The Well of the Saints* took shape, I realized that every character in the play from the Saint to Timmy the

Smith was bad-tempered right through the play, hence, as I pointed out to Synge, all this bad temper would inevitably infect the audience and make them bad-tempered too. I suggested that the Saint anyway might be made into a good-natured easy-going man, or that Molly Byrne might be made a loveable young girl, but Synge would not budge. He said he wanted to write 'like a monochrome painting, all in shades of the one colour'. I argued that all drama depended on contrast and on tension. All in vain. We had to agree to differ.

One technical trouble we had to overcome was that Synge had not yet acquired the art of breaking up his dialogue into short speeches, without which it is impossible for the actors to get pace. Many of his speeches were very long. They took a cruel lot of practice before we could get them spoken at a reasonably good pace and without at the same time losing the lovely lilt of the idiom.

W. G. Fay, *The Fays of the Abbey Theatre*
(London: Rich and Cowan, 1935), p. 166-9

[While the play was in rehearsal the text was prepared for publication. Yeats was invited to contribute a Preface, in which he discusses Synge's dramaturgy and certain visual aspects of the production.]

Every writer, even every small writer, who has belonged to the great tradition, has had his dream of an impossibly noble life, and the greater he is, the more does it seem to plunge him into some beautiful or bitter reverie. Some, and of these are all the earliest poets of the world, gave it direct expression; others mingle it so subtly with reality that it is a day's work to disentangle it; others bring it near by showing us whatever is most its contrary. Mr. Synge, indeed, sets before us ugly, deformed, or sinful people, but his people, moved by no practical ambition, are driven by a dream of that impossible life. That we may feel how intensely his Woman of the Glen dreams of days that shall be entirely alive, she that is a 'hard woman to please' must spend her days between a sour-faced old husband, a man who goes mad upon the hills, a craven lad and a drunken tramp; and those two blind people of *The Well of the Saints* are so transformed by the dream that they choose blindness rather than reality. He tells us of realities, but he knows that art has never taken more than its symbols from anything that the eye can see or the hand measure.

It is the preoccupation of his characters with their dream that gives his plays their drifting movement, their emotional subtlety. In most of the dramatic writing of our time, and this is one of the reasons why our dramatists do not find the need for a better speech, one finds a simple motive lifted, as it were, into the full light of the stage. The ordinary student of drama will not find anywhere in *The Well of the Saints* that

45

excitement of the will in the presence of attainable advantages, which he is accustomed to think the natural stuff of drama, and if he see it played he will wonder why act is knitted to act so loosely, why it is all like a decoration on a flat surface, why there is so much leisure in the dialogue, even in the midst of passion.

While I write, we are rehearsing *The Well of the Saints,* and are painting for it decorative scenery, mountains in one or two flat colours and without detail, ash-trees and red salleys with something of recurring pattern in their woven boughs. For though the people of the play use no phrase they could not use in daily life, we know that we are seeking to express what no eye has ever seen.

W. B. Yeats, Abbey Theatre, 27 January 1905

[During rehearsals Joseph Holloway wrote to Fay urging him to amend Synge's text. His diary entry of 11 January reads: 'J. M. Synge conducted the rehearsal . . . and although he has made some cuts in the text much yet remains to be erased before an Irish audience is likely to swallow it. Parts of it suggest to the mind a picturesque setting of the slang dictionary. . . . Having written so far, a thought struck me to drop a line of warning to Frank J. Fay re the matter, and this was the result. . . . Dear Mr. Fay, Just a word in your ear as a sincere friend and well-wisher of the Irish National Theatre Society. Please use all your power to have certain passages, such as that about the priest and the pair in the ditch, and the two or three coarse references to bringing all sorts of monstrosities into the world, indulged in by the Douls and Timmy the Smith, erased from *The Well of the Saints.* For, if they are allowed to remain they will undoubtedly give unnecessary offence to most of those who witness the play, and probably ruin the Society's chance of future success in Dublin. Billingsgate no matter how clothed in imagery of diabolical cleverness remains Billingsgate and never can become anything else; and when linked with irreverence it becomes quite intolerable to an Irish audience. Be warned by me, who knows the pulse of audiences fairly well by this time, and cut as much of the nastiness as possible out of the piece. Having said so much, as a sincere friend, I leave the rest to your good sense to see my warning fall not on deaf ears . . .'. Fay's reply started: 'Thanks for your kind letter. I cannot help thinking that you are needlessly alarmed over *The Well of the Saints.* Surely a Dublin public who crowd to hear *The Geisha* and the other musical comedies full of eroticism conveyed to the audience by that subtle minister music, who go to *Faust* and revel in *Tristan and Isolde,* to say nothing of Shakespeare, will not be affronted when they hear two or three people on our stage speaking after their kind. You must close your ears to the language of our city if you think Irish people don't say such things; and I personally like plain speaking. It is only suggestion that does harm' (*The Abbey Theatre: the Years of Synge, 1905-1907*, p. 16-17). Holloway, however, was nearer the mark.]

The point of view is not that of a writer in sympathetic touch with the people from whom he purports to draw his characters. To begin with, he knows nothing of Irish peasant religion. The widow in *Riders to the Sea,* who consoles herself with the thought that her prayers to Providence may cease, leaves off her praying just when the Irish peasant's prayers would really begin. The wife in *The Shadow of the Glen* shows never a trace of the conscience that even the vagabond carries somewhere in Ireland. With Martin Doul — the principal character, in fact, the only character in *The Well of the Saints* — religion is only a decayed mythology, useful for incantation or imprecation, but having no further concern with soul or body. Behind this representation of the popular religion is the subtle irony of the latter-day French school satirizing a Providence that has ceased to be paternal, and is shadowed forth merciless as the Destiny of the Greek drama. Such a presentation of the peasant religion, lacking in reverence and expressed in a jargon of profane familiarity, is an artistic blunder and a constant offence. Again Mr. Synge is as preoccupied with the sex problem as any of the London school of problem playwrights. . . . Add to all this, or rather a result of all this, Mr. Synge's leading characters repel sympathy. . . . The analysis of the blind man's feelings and frenzies is not without power; and in the dialogue beauty of thought and felicity of phrase are not lacking. The monologue of the lonely blind man after darkness has fallen upon him a second time is quite searching in its pathos. But the roughness of the peasants' passion is exaggerated, the ferocity of their rage excessive, and the hell-wrath of their imprecations repulsive. . . . The players did excellently in the measure of their opportunity. Mr. W. G. Fay is a comedian of rare powers, and in the subtler touches of his part was excellent. His explosions were not convincing, but that, perhaps, was not his fault. Miss Emma Vernon as the blind woman was also admirable. Her brogue is perfect, and the peasant manner is given without strain or stiffness. The other characters afforded the actors little chance; but Mr. George Roberts's Timmy, the Smith, was made the most of and Mr. F. J. Fay as a wandering Friar gave as much reality and sincerity to the part as could be put in it.

The Freeman's Journal, 6 Feb. 1905, p. 5

It is, we know, heresy to suggest an amplification of the scenery. That, it is said, would unduly distract attention from the literary matter, but there were periods during the performance of Saturday when a little distraction from the long-drawn dialogues would have been a relief. . . . Saturday's play was particularly crude in its scenic equipment. It was a three act play, and in the first and last the background was a tolerably well-painted mountain, reminiscent more of the west than the east of Ireland.

The Irish Times, 6 Feb. 1905, p. 71

The most serious defect in Mr. Synge's play is that it is more than doubtful whether in any part of Ireland are to be found such types of the Irish peasant as Martin and Mary Doul, who, as far as I can see, have nothing to recommend them. The old type of whiskey-drinking, jig-dancing, handy, rascal Irishman manifested a certain boisterous and somewhat objectionable vivacity in and out of season — mostly out — but I question if in most respects he was not greatly the superior of the pessimistic loafer which there is a tendency to set up as the standard.

The Evening Herald, 6 Feb. 1905, p. 3

The story — a well known one — has been treated in our own time by an English novelist. Mr. Synge's localization of it is a failure, and his dramatization disappointing. His peasants are not Irish, and the language they use in strife is pure Whitechapel. The dialogue is most uneven, varying from passages of lyric beauty to violent eruptions of no real strength; the duologues are lengthy, iterative, and apt to become wearisome. The imperfections of the play are numerous, and it is dragged out to three times its natural length. A moment of possible fine tragedy when Martin Doul recovers his sight is overlooked by the author, and the blunder by which he confounds the loss of sight with the loss of imagination is so gross that even the 'Theatre of Commerce' cannot produce its equal. One of the most amusing blunders which the author perpetrates is making the blind man immediately on recovering his sight recognize people by the colour of their hair. The atmosphere of the play is harsh, unsympathetic, and at the same time sensual. Its note of utter hopelessness evokes a feeling akin to compassion for the author. What there is 'Irish', 'national,' or 'dramatic' about it even Oedipus might fail to solve. How is it that the Irish National Theatre, which started so well, can now only alternate a decadent wail with a Calvinistic groan.

Arthur Griffith, 'All Ireland', *The United Irishman*, 11 Feb. 1905, p. 1

[Arthur Griffith, above, was predictably hostile, but support for Synge, came from an unexpected quarter. George Moore wrote the following in a letter to the Editor of *The Irish Times*.]

I should like to call the attention of the readers of *The Irish Times* to an important event which has just happened in Dublin, and which very likely may be overlooked by them and to their great regret hereafter. The event I allude to is of exceeding rarity, it happens occasionally in Paris. I have never seen in London any play written originally in English that I can look upon as dramatic literature. I have not forgotten Oscar Wilde's plays — that delicious comedy *The Importance of Being Earnest* — but however much I admire them I cannot forget that their style is derived from that of Restoration comedy, whereas Mr. Synge's little play seems to me to be of a new growth. . . . I would call attention to the abundance and the beauty of the dialogue, to the fact that one listens to it as one listens to music and the ease with which phrase is linked into phrase. At every moment the dialogue seems to lose itself, but it finds its way out. Mr. Synge has discovered great literature in barbarous idiom as gold is discovered in quartz, and to do such a thing is surely a rare literary achievement.

The interpretation partakes of the literary quality, it is original and it is like itself. Mr. W. Fay was wholly admirable as the blind beggar, he was whimsical and insolent, and pathetic in turn; he was always in the key, and his love scene with Molly Byrne seemed to me a little triumph of distinguished acting. The close of the act was especially effective in intonation and in gesture. Mr. Frank Fay was very good as the saint, the part is a difficult one, and the ecclesiastical note might not have been caught as well by another actor. The part of the blind beggarwoman was so well played by Miss Vernon that I am afraid I shall regret having spoken of it, for I shall not find words wherewith to praise it enough. Above all I admired her reticence, and it seemed to me that she must have thought the part out from end to end, omitting nothing that might be omitted. The age of the old woman is portrayed in every gesture, the walk and the bodily stiffness, and something of the mind of an old woman, for in her voice there is a certain mental stiffness. Her elocution was faultless. Some will say that she was not effective enough when she left the church, but I do not share this opinion. I think in seeking to be effective she would have been less true.

George Moore, letter to *The Irish Times*, 13 Feb. 1905, p. 6

[Holloway maintained his position and recorded on 11 February: 'Mr. Synge, I believe, was not present at the performance on Friday night, and I happened to be in the Green Room on Saturday when he made his appearance and Lady Gregory asked him, 'What happened to you last night? We thought you had committed suicide!' Which was the severest thing said of him or his play in my hearing during the week from one of the worshippers. Oh it was shocking!' He goes on to say: 'I have never witnessed a play that repelled me so much as this same *Well of the Saints* written by one who has as much sympathy for the humbler Irish and their Catholic faith as a Maxim gun with an Englishman at the side of it has for a lot of unarmed savages! It raised my gall every time I saw it' (*Joseph Holloway's Abbey Theatre*, p. 54).

In *The Fays of the Abbey Theatre* Willie Fay sums up his feeling about the play's reception: 'As before, few of our public knew what to make of it. Was it a piece of harsh realism or was there something else behind it? The lyrical speeches were beyond them, and there was the old suspicion that most of the plays we produced were intended in some way to debunk the saintly Irish character. . . . In short the play was admired and enjoyed by those who were capable of regarding it simply as a play without reading into it a criticism of the Irish people or an attack on their religion. But these were too few. The great majority, thinking of religion and themselves, abominated the play on both counts. It had a bad press and we lost money' (p. 169).

The Well of the Saints was translated into German as early as 1905, by Max Meyerfeld, and this German version was produced by Max Reinhardt's Deutsches Theater in Berlin in January 1906, but was not a success. The play was, however, well-received in London, where it was described as 'perhaps the most humorous, the bitterest, and the most beautiful of Synge's plays'.]

Synge's *The Well of the Saints* was beautiful to read, and proves extraordinarily stimulating on the stage. In this little play Synge shows the power, common to all great creative work, of transfiguring his material, of seeing things and making us see things as though they were newly created. The words used last night are possible peasant utterance, but we are not to suppose that the author took a victoria to see the peasants, as one French realist said of another, or that the play is a verbatim transcript of the jottings of a note-book. The talk of these poor folk comes to us through the artist, that saving wall between us and a so-called realism. The theme is brutal enough for any realist — the healing by a saint of a pair of blind beggars, the man's revulsion at the revealed ugliness of his wife, his desire for the first beautiful woman he sees, her contempt and rejection of him, the old couple's miserable compromise. Zola would have given you every cut of their soiled feet, every horror of their rags, every dark place in their souls. Synge walks the road in fellowship with them. His is creative work, and the angels of heaven, the pigsty, the common muck of the road, the passions of men and women are all assimilated with equal zest and given back to us with the old relative value as between each other, but of new and equal loveliness in his exquisite and self-conscious prose. . . . It is English as elaborately found, for all its artlessness, as Flaubert's French.

And Synge does for his people what he has done for their speech. The theme is no longer ignoble, squalid, mean. When Martin Doul, inarticulate poet in real life, articulate only when he speaks through Synge, leaves the church healed, and makes his way to the beautfiul Molly Byrne, shrinking instinctively from the hag in whom he does not recognize his wife, the audience laughed a little — audiences always laugh a little — although the thing is pitiful. His belief in the continued loveliness of his wife has been the blind old man's comfort. The lie always comfortably maintained by the village is exposed, and Martin is torn between loathing of his wife and desire of the beautiful woman. Zola would have shown the animal; Synge shows the poison of disillusion, the inveterate poet in the man going out to the first loveliness he has known, and, perhaps strongest of all, the horror of old age and the imminence of decay. 'It's a few sees the old women rotting for the grave.' It would be a mistake to imagine that the play is all high tragedy or even tearful. There is extraordinary comic bite to much of it and a deal of honest laughter. Merciful darkness falls upon the old couple again, and they realize, he that he will have a glorious white beard, she that she will have soft white hair the way there won't be the like of her in the seven counties of the east. 'Sight's a queer thing for upsetting a man', they decide, declining the offer of a second healing. . . .

James Agate, 'The Irish Players',
Buzz, Buzz! Essays on the Theatre (London, 1917), p. 153-6.

[*The Well of the Saints* was also successful when the Abbey production visited New York, marking the first performance of a Synge play in America. The cast included three celebrated Irish actors: Arthur Sinclair as Martin, Sara Allgood as Mary, and Maire O'Neill as Molly.]

New York last night had its first stage glimpse of a Synge play. The play was *The Well of the Saints*, an interesting, poetic, and, if you like, symbolic work, although perhaps not one of its author's very best. Still it is characteristic of Synge and his way of looking at humans and the powers of living custom, living tradition, and of superstition which is very much alive. . . . The three acts in which this tale is unfolded reveal some traits of a world, a peasant world, which, as Synge says, is as yet unspoiled for the poet and the poetic dramatist. These people are people among whom he lived, lived intimately and with perceptions bared. He treasured, with memory and notes, their turns of speech, the rich mines of their folk lore, and the depths and sensitiveness of their spirit, and he is interpreted by players who understand him and who understand them.

New York Daily Tribune, 24 Nov. 1911

[In 1932, again in New York but in an inappropriate auditorium, Brooks Atkinson praised the play while lamenting the inadequacy of the acting company. He recognized the demands of the text and the need for a trained ensemble to realize its complexities.]

Having no place to lay its head, the Irish Theatre has tucked Synge's *The*

Well of the Saints into a luxuriously appointed assembly-room at the Barbizon, where Augustin Duncan and a company appeared last evening. No setting could be more hostile to a richly poetic comedy of a lonely mountainous district in Ireland. And except for the acting of Mr. Duncan, P. J. Kelly, and Agnes McGrath, the performance has none of the dance and racial fervour that must lie at the roots of this fertile play. . . . Mr. Duncan, who has been blind these several years, plays the beggar with that wholeness of artistic understanding, that love of music, and that certainty of acting technique that have endeared him to all who know his high place in the theatre. Although he is a blind man, playing the part of a blind man in a drama, he illuminates his part with the seeing mind of an artist. . . . As the blind beggar's blind wife, Miss McGrath has the flowing intonation of phrasing that brings the colour to Synge's dialogue and Mr. Kelly, as the holy father, gives his lines the resonance of good speaking. But three good actors set down in the midst of an uninspired performance and suavely tucked away into the corner of a modern hotel, do not bring a Synge play to life. *The Well of the Saints* has compassion, love of humanity, and a faith in the poetic ideal that only a trained company could engender.

J. Brooks Atkinson, *New York Times*, 22 Jan. 1932

[The Irish production seen again by Agate in London in 1943 had no such shortcomings. In it William Fay re-created the role of Martin almost forty years after the play's premiere.]

Synge's piece still remains the little masterpiece it always was, full of humour, irony, pathos, and wonderful poetry. . . . This exquisite little piece has pattern, which today's film-fed playgoer will surely relegate to the limbo of craftsmanship. A beautiful performance of Martin by Mr. W. G. Fay, and a nice one of Mary by Miss Maureen Moore.

James Agate, *Sunday Times*, 21 Mar.1943

[Hugh Hunt, later to become the Artistic Director of the Abbey Theatre, directed the play in 1954 in a production which caused reviewers to re-assess the position of *The Playboy* as Synge's 'best' play.]

For all its poetry and the miracle from which its tale proceeds, *The Well of the Saints* is a work of cruel realism. Nowhere is there expressed more brutally the sense that many must have, in middle-age, of having made the wrong marriage. But whereas in life the apprehension of failure comes gradually and has all manner of alleviations, such as custom, patience, humour, and some notion that others are in the same plight, on the stage it is represented as instantaneous and appalling. At one moment the blind couple, long deluded by their neighbours into believing themselves still young to look at and possessed of a beauty neither ever had, are devotedly happy. The next, the sight taken from them in childhood miraculously restored, both are cursing the Providence that, in a world full of golden lads and girls, chose for each a companion so ill-favoured. Since Synge was a humorist as well as a poet and a moralist, their preoccupation with beauty makes their fellow-villagers uneasy, and sturdy confident fellows like Timmy the Smith begin to be self-conscious. There is, of course, a great deal more in the play than this, and an excellent Irish company discloses a good deal of it. Mr. Liam Redmond and Miss Peggy Marshall are the Douls near enough, and Miss Sheila Manahan the heartless Molly Byrne.

The Times, 28 April 1954

[In New York at the Gaiety Theatre on 10 April 1959, the play was revived in a double bill with Lady Gregory's *The Workhouse Ward*.]

Although the plays are by different hands and have different themes, it is fascinating to observe the qualities they have in common. In the first place, the prose has a melodious phrasing. Synge was the great composer in words. But Lady Gregory's trifle also has rhythm, tone, and colour.

In the second place, both plays are monoclastic. What is normal is what is unbearable. In the third place, the characters are rugged individualists. Each one has a good opinion of himself and a low opinion of the others. Like most of the characters in the great period of Abbey Theatre drama, they are peasants, and they are scornful of one another — vigorous, hard-headed, sharp-tongued, alert, irascible under the flowing imagery of the dialogue.

Under the direction of Louis Beachner, the performance is simple but lively. The actors do not try to imitate Irish speech, but they are aware of the rich style and the music that is concentrated within. . . . Frederick Koestler's utilitarian settings and Ben Morse's village costumes provide a sufficient if uninventive production. But it is the original Irish mind and the Irish literary style of a half-century ago that gives this theatre event its tang. The freshness of Synge and Lady Gregory has lost none of its irony and bubble.

Brooks Atkinson, *New York Times*, 11 Apr. 1959

[In August 1970, Hugh Hunt's Abbey production played at the Old Vic, London, to great critical acclaim. Robert Cushman described it as 'a disturbing experience' (*The Spectator*, 5 Aug 1970), and Michael Billington's review, below, is representative of the critical approval for this memorable production. It also points out the need, in modern times, to emphasize the inherent realism of the play and, as Synge said himself to his Abbey actors, that sense should never be subordinate to musicality.]

John Millington Synge was a curiously paradoxical figure: an urban Protestant bourgeois who wrote truly affectionate studies of the rural Catholic lower-classes. With his use of an exquisite, rhythmic, self-conscious prose, he is naturally somewhat out of fashion at the moment but, as this Abbey Theatre production shows, his best work still has a moving simplicity and strength.

Although Synge has no love for late nineteenth-century naturalism, in this play he comes curiously close to the spirit of Ibsen. The theme is that of illusion versus reality: in particular, the need for the human imagination to create a new world once one's original illusions have been shattered. The message is embodied in a simple fable about a blind couple who, when granted their sight, find all their cherished beliefs about each other and the external world crumbling away. Consequently, when their blindness returns, they gratefully accept it as a liberation and spurn the offer of divine assistance to have their sight restored.

The most welcome feature of Hugh Hunt's production is its avoidance of the Synge-song that can turn each of this dramatist's convoluted sentences into a miniature operatic aria: sense rightly comes before sound. There is also no attempt to invest the situation with a spurious sentimentality, and the ferocious intolerance both of the blind couple themselves and of the village community that stones them for their ingratitude is heavily underlined. However some rather cumbersome grouping — with too many solid peasant figures planted downstage — obscures some of the most powerful theatrical moments such as the blind peasant's first recognition of the faces around him after his miraculous healing.

To a modern audience the trickiest feature of the play is accepting the miracles so easily performed by a rough travelling saint: all the more credit, therefore, to John Kavanagh for endowing this Christ-like figure with a serene authority that conceals a vein of angry impatience. Eamon Kelly and Maire Ni Dhomhnail as the afflicted twosome also eschew easy pathos and provide a genuine portrait of flinty peasant indomitability.

Michael Billington, *The Guardian*, 5 Aug. 1970

The Playboy of the Western World

A comedy in three acts.
Written: 1906.
First production: National Theatre Society, Abbey Theatre, Dublin, 26 Jan. 1907 (dir. W. G. Fay, who also played Christy Mahon; with Arthur Sinclair as Michael James, Maire O'Neill as Pegeen Mike, F. J. Fay as Shawn Keogh, and Sara Allgood as the Widow Quin).

Published: Dublin: Maunsel, 1907; *The Works of John M. Synge,
Volume II* (Dublin: Maunsel, 1910); *Collected Works, Volume IV:
Plays, Book 2* (Oxford University Press, 1968); with *Riders to the
Sea,* Oxford: Basil Blackwell, 1969; Dublin: Mercier Press, 1969;
Complete Plays (London: Methuen, 1981); Methuen Student Edition,
1983; *Plays, Poems, and Prose* (London: Dent, 1992).

*A young man arrives at a little public-house and tells the
publican's daughter that he has murdered his father. He so tells
it that he has all her sympathy, and every time he retells it, with
new exaggeration and additions, he wins the sympathy of
somebody or other, for it is the countryman's habit to be against
the law. The countryman thinks the more terrible the crime, the
greater must the provocation have been. The young man himself,
under the excitement of his own story, becomes gay, energetic
and lucky. He prospers in love, comes in first at the local races,
and bankrupts the roulette tables afterwards. Then the father
arrives with his head bandaged but very lively, and the people
turn upon the impostor. To win back their esteem he takes up a
spade to kill his father in earnest, but, horrified at the threat of
what had sounded so well in the story, they bind him to hand
over to the police. The father releases him and father and son
walk off together, the son, still buoyed up by his imagination,
announcing that he will be master henceforth.*

W. B. Yeats, *Autobiographies*, p. 569-70

[Synge started *Playboy* in 1905. Yeats wrote to him from London: 'I am
looking forward to your new play with great expectations. There are
very stirring rumours about your first act' (8 July). But owing to
frequent periods of illness he was unable to work properly until the
following year. On 5 August he wrote to Lady Gregory: 'I am pleased
with the way my play is going but I find it is quite impossible to rush
through with it now, so I rather think I shall take it and the typewriter to
Kerry where I could work. By doing so I would get some sort of holiday
and still avoid dropping the play again — which is a rather dangerous
process.' The production was eventually scheduled for 19 December,
but on 4 October Synge, back in Dublin, wrote to Yeats: 'My play,
though in its last agony, is not finished and I cannot promise it for any
definite day. It is more than likely that when I read it to you and Fay.
there will be little things to alter that have escaped me. And with my
stuff it takes time to get even half a page of new dialogue fully into key

with what goes before it. The play, I think, will be one of the longest we have done, and in places extremely difficult . . . '. During November he wrote to Lady Gregory: 'I have only very little now to do to the *Playboy* to get him *provisionally* finished' (5 Nov.), and to Yeats: 'I would have been in during the week but I could not leave the *Playboy*. I am nearly in distraction with him, and consequently am very unwell.' But on 8 November he wrote to Lady Gregory: 'May I read the *Playboy* to you and Yeats and Fay some time tomorrow, Saturday or Monday according as it suits you all. A little verbal correction is still necessary and one or two structural points may need — I fancy do need — revision, but I would like to have your opinion on it before I go further.' The reading took place on 13 November, but only of Acts I and II. Lady Gregory was encouraging: 'We are longing to have the last act of *Playboy*. We were both immensely impressed and delighted with the play' (16 Nov.).

After further revision the play went into rehearsal on 8 January 1907, with the opening scheduled for 26 January. Synge reported that he was in an 'anxious state'. Problems arose in rehearsal over the strong language, and Synge reluctantly made some cuts. He complained to his friend Jack Yeats, who responded in a letter: 'If you don't want to have to leave out all the coloured language in your play you'll have to station a drummer in the wings, to welt the drums every time the language gets too high for the stomachs of the audience. They used to do this in the music halls' (11 Jan.). Synge's anxiety was heightened by his concern over the cast's ability to embrace and perform in the appropriate style. He attended rehearsals regularly, causing Lady Gregory to remark to Yeats: 'You have never looked like a tiger with its cub as Synge did last night with *Playboy*.' Just before opening night she wrote to Synge: 'I am sure *Playboy* will go all right. One always gets nervous towards the end — they seemed to me as if they could not go wrong with it' (*Our Irish Theatre*, p. 130-2). Synge replied on the day of the first performance: 'Thanks for your note. . . . I do not know how things will go tonight, the day company are all very steady, but Power is in a most deplorable state of uncertainty. Miss O'Sullivan and [Miss] Craig are very shaky also on the few words they have to speak. . . . I have a sort [of] second edition of influenza, and I am looking gloomily at everything. Fay has worked very hard all through and everything has gone smoothly' (26 Jan.). Willie Fay, who directed and played Christy Mahon, gives his account of the production process and his dealings with Synge.]

He would not forgive the crass ignorance, the fatuity, the malevolence with which *The Well of the Saints* had been received. He had given of his best in good faith, and offence had been taken where no offence had been intended. 'Very well then', he said to me bitterly one night, 'the next play I write I will make sure will annoy them. . . . And he did. As soon as I cast eyes over the script of *The Playboy of the Western World* I knew we were in for serious trouble unless he would consent to alter it drastically.

Many and many a time I strove with him, using all arguments I could muster, to get him to see that if you attack your audience you must expect them to retaliate, that you might as well write to a newspaper and expect the editor not to insist on the last word. The emotions displayed on the stage are designed by the author, and interpreted by the players to give the audience a vicarious experience of them, and if the audience reacts to them, that is the measure of the author's and actors' success. Thus, laughter on the stage makes laughter in the house and anger makes anger. But by laughter I mean, straight laughter, not wrath disguised in a grain which the average audience is quick to see through and resent accordingly. Synge could never be made to understand that. He was apt to think in the terms of Zola, who got his effects by keeping all his characters in one key. He would never see that Zola was a novelist, not a dramatist, and that there is all the difference between a printed story that one reads to oneself and the same story told as a play to a mixed audience of varying degrees of intelligence.

Frank and I begged him to make Pegeen a decent likeable country girl, which she might easily have been without injury to the play, and to take out the torture scene in the last act where the peasants burn Christy with the lit turf. It was no use referring him to all the approved rules of the theatrical game — that, for example, while a note of comedy was admirable for heightening tragedies the converse was not true. The things that we wanted him to alter did not amount to five per cent of the whole play. *The Well of the Saints* had suffered from too much anger. *The Playboy of the Western World* was anger *in excelsis*. The characters were as fine and diverting a set of scallywags as one could invent for one story, but it was years too soon for our audiences to appreciate them as dramatic creations.

Frank and I might as well have saved our breath. We might as well have tried to move the Hill of Howth as move Synge. That was his play, he said, and, barring one or two jots and tittles of 'bad language' that he grudgingly consented to excise, it was the play that with a great screwing up of courage we produced.

I gave the *Playboy* long and careful rehearsal, doing my best to tone down the bitterness of it, and all the time with a sinking heart I knew we were in for trouble, but it was my business to get Synge's play produced as nearly to his notions as possible in the circumstances and with the material at my disposal.

W. G. Fay, *The Fays of the Abbey Theatre*, p. 211-13

[The first reviews praised the acting and certain sections of the play, but condemned the strong language. The following is fairly representative.]

Expectation was raised to a high pitch in anticipation of the production of another new play by an Irish writer, one who has made his mark in the repertoire of the National Theatre Society. . . . The characters in the play are drawn from the people of the west of Ireland, and their language and methods of expression are as simple, unadorned, and direct as those of one type which they purport to represent. The comedy is in three acts, which are neither long nor heavy, and the dialogue is in many parts sparkling and witty. It would, perhaps, be the better for some slight revision here and there, particularly in the third act in which there is a sentence spoken by the hero, which gave rise to an emphatic expression of dissent from the gallery, and which nobody could say was not justified. . . . Mr. W. G. Fay invests the part of Christy Mahon with that touch of humour which he knows so well how to impart to it. The part of Margaret Flaherty is quite a good one, and Miss Mary O'Neill displayed her undoubted power in impersonating the publican's good-looking daughter. Mr. Arthur Sinclair's make-up, as the bucolic publican, was admirable, as his return home next morning from the 'wake' somewhat 'under the influence' was suitable to the occasion. The Widow Quin plays a prominent part in the story of this playboy, Christy. She is his most persistent suitor, and her role is probably the most comical in the whole piece. Miss Sara Allgood, shawled and coiffed in the manner of the western peasant women, fulfilled the part to perfection. . . . The first act is brilliant and witty in dialogue and it made an excellent impression on the audience. The two following acts did not, however, quite maintain the standards thus set up, and the final curtain descended leaving many persons dissatisfied with the denouement. The incident already referred to — the howl set up at the objectionable phrase given to Christy to speak — spoiled everyone's chance of appreciating the finish of what is, on the whole, a clever piece of writing, cleverly acted and appropriately staged.

The Daily Express, 28 Jan. 1907

[*The Freeman's Journal* called the play an 'unmitigated, protracted libel upon Irish peasant men and, worse still, upon Irish peasant girlhood. . . . It is quite plain that there is a need for a censor at the Abbey Theatre.' 'Jacques' of *The Independent* commented on Christy: 'His language, his garb, and his actions may excite laughter in some, but it was a tribute to the good taste and common sense of the audience that hissing and booing mingled with the cheers which greeted the final development of the character that, let us hope, exists only in the lively imagination of the author.' *The Evening Mail* entitled its review 'A Dramatic Freak' and dismissed the plot as 'absurd and un-Irish. . . . [It] smacks of the decadent ideas of the literary flaneurs of Paris rather than of simple Connaught.' And *The Irish Times* observed: 'Mr. Synge, we are afraid, must to some extent sacrifice the "remorseless truth" if his play is to be made acceptable to healthy public opinion.' There was particular objection to the use of the word 'shift'. In a letter to *The Freeman's Journal* a correspondent claiming to be 'A Western Girl' cited it as 'a word indicating an essential item of female attire, which the lady would probably never utter in ordinary circumstances, even to herself.' Lady Gregory telegraphed to Yeats, who was in Scotland at the time: 'Audience broke up in disorder at the word shift.' Synge wrote to Molly after the first performance.]

I wish I had you here to talk over the whole show last night. W. G. [Fay] was pretty bluffy, and Power was very confused in places. Then the crowd was wretched and Mrs. W. G. [Brigit O'Dempsey] missed the new cue we gave, though she can hardly be blamed for that. I think with a better Mahon and crowd and a few slight cuts the play would be thoroughly sound. I feel like old Maurya today, 'It's four fine plays I have, though it was a hard birth I had with every one of them and they coming to the world.'

It is better any day to have the row we had last night, than to have your play fizzling out in half-hearted applause. Now we'll be talked about. We're an event in the history of the Irish stage.

Synge, *Letters to Molly*, ed. Ann Saddlemyer
(Oxford University Press, 1971), p. 87-8

[It is clear from this letter that Synge was not aware how deeply he had offended the audience. The 'row' was to grow during the days ahead until the 'event' turned into the celebrated 'Playboy Riots'. Willie Fay describes one of the performances.]

The first act went splendidly, and I was beginning to feel hopeful, even cheerful. The second act, too, opened to plenty of laughter. We had not got to the begining of the 'rough stuff'. But with the entrance of the Widow Quin the audience began to show signs of restlessness. Obviously they couldn't abide her; and when we came to my line about 'all bloody fool', the trouble began in earnest, with hisses and cat-calls, and all the other indications that the audience are not in love with you. Now that word 'bloody' in the script had given me qualms, but Synge had insisted — and who was I to contradict him? — that in the West it was the casual mild expletive, like 'bally', or 'beastly' or 'bloomin', Yet how was Dublin to know that? In Dublin, as for that matter all over England and Scotland in those days, it was a 'low' word, a poorhouse word. Quite a lot of years later, even, it provided the theatrical sensation of the London season when Bernard Shaw's Eliza Doolittle rapped it out in *Pygmalion*. Nowadays, I understand, it is so much a young lady's expression that no he-man ever dreams of using it. Synge was in advance of his time. There was therefore some excuse for the audiences protest, though it was needlessly violent. Yet the queer thing was that what turned the audience into a veritable mob of howling devils was not this vulgar expletive, but as irreproachable a word as there is in the English dictionary — the decent old-fashioned 'shift' for the traditional under-garment of a woman. There is a point in the play where Christy (which in this case was poor me) says, 'It's Pegeen I'm seeking only, and what'd I care if you brought me a drift of chosen females standing in their shifts itself, maybe from this place to the Eastern World.' You may say that the image — a magnificent one, mark you — must have been shocking to so unsophisticated an audience as ours, but it was not the image that shocked them. It was the word, for the row was just as bad when Pegeen Mike herself said to the Widow Quin, 'Is it you asking for a penn'orth of starch, with ne'er a shift or a shirt as long as you can remember?'

The last act opened with the house in an uproar, and by the time the curtain fell, the uproar had become a riot. Two or three times I tried to get them to let us finish for the sake of those who wanted to hear the play, but it was no use. They wanted a row and they were going to have one. There were free fights in the stalls. Mr. Hills, our conductor, got his face damaged, and at one time it seemed as if the stage would be stormed. . . . It was lucky for themselves that the patriots did not venture as far as that, for our call-boy, who was also boiler attendant and general factotum, had armed himself with a big axe from the boiler-room, and swore by all the saints in the calendar that he would chop the head off the first lad who came over the footlights. And knowing him, I haven't a shadow of a doubt that he would have chopped.

This was on a Saturday night. Over Sunday the directors had to consider whether they would bow to the storm and withdraw the play, or face it out. Very properly they took the courageous course, and the company, though it was no joke for them, loyally supported their decision to go on playing at all costs. And so on the Monday night the curtain was rung up to a well-organized pandemonium, for the patriots had been busy over the weekend also. As it was impossible for any of us to be heard, I arranged with the cast that we should simply walk through the play, not speaking a word aloud, but changing positions and going through all the motions, so to speak. The house was terrific, but we finished the play. It was not until the Thursday night that, in order to give a fair deal to those who had paid money to hear, the directors had the police in the theatre. We also had taken the precaution to pad the floor with felt, which frustrated the rhythmic stamping that had been the opposition's most effective device. Thus we were able once more to speak the lines, but our reputation as an Irish national institution was ruined. Not content with libelling the saintly Irish people, we had actually called in the tyrant Saxon myrmidons to silence their righteous indignation! Of course the root of the trouble was that Synge had written a brilliant play about the Irish peasantry without any of the traditional sentiment or illusions that were then so dear to the Irish playgoer. He was accused of making a deliberate attack on the national character, whatever that may be. . . .

W. G. Fay, *The Fays of the Abbey Theatre*, p. 214-17

[Yeats tried to contain the uproar by offering a formal platform for debate. He made the following speech from the stage of the Abbey after a performance of *Riders to the Sea* which preceded *Playboy*, and was always received with the utmost respect.]

A difference of opinion has arisen between the management of this theatre and some of the audience as to the value of the play which we are now to produce, and as to our policy in producing it. If any of you wish to discuss the merits of the play or our rightness in producing it, I shall be delighted to discuss it with you, and do my best to answer your arguments. I will endeavour to get an audience, and invite any who wish to speak to come on the stage to do so. . . . On Monday evening I shall be pleased to hear you. We have put this play before you to be heard and to be judged, as every play should be heard and judged. Every man has a right to hear it and condemn it if he pleases, but no man has a right to interfere with another man hearing a play and judging for himself . . . The country that condescends either to bully or to permit itself to be bullied soon ceases to have any fine qualities, and I promise you that if there is any small section in this theatre that wish to deny the right of others to hear what they themselves don't want to hear . . . we will play on, and our patience shall last longer than their patience. . . .

'The Abbey Theatre', *The Daily Express* (Dublin),
30 Jan. 1907, p. 5

[Yeats's offer did nothing to dispel the commotion, however, and the pandemonium continued. It was fuelled by an interview with Synge which appeared in the *Dublin Evening Mail* on 29 January.]

Mr. Synge, who had promised me half an hour after the play was over, was scarcely in a mood for being interviewed. He looked excited and restless, the perspiration standing out in great beads over his forehead and cheeks, and besides, he seemed just then in extraordinary demand by sundry persons, who had all sorts of things to say to him. . . . We were continually jostled and interrupted, . . . but I was not going to grumble. I was conscious of the one thing only — that I had cornered my man, and must have it out with him. . . . 'Tell me, Mr. Synge, was your purpose in writing this play to represent Irish life as it is lived — in short, did you think yourself holding up the mirror to nature?'

'No, no', Mr. Synge answered, rather emphatically. . . . 'What, then, was your object in this play?' I asked after a while.

'Nothing', Mr. Synge answered, with sustained emphasis, due probably to his excited condition, 'simply the idea appealed to me — it pleased myself, and I worked it up.'

'But do you see now how it displeases others? And did you ever think, when writing it, how it would be received by the public?'

'I never thought of it. . . . I wrote the play because it pleased me, and it just happens that I know Irish life best, so I made my methods Irish.'

'Then', I interposed, 'the real truth is you had no idea of catering for the Irish National Theatre. The main idea of the play pleased your own artistic sense, and that gave it an Irish setting as a mere accident, owing to your intimate knowledge of Irish life.' 'Exactly so', he answered.

I paused for a moment to reflect upon this new tenet in art. In idealistic quarters it has ever been the cry, art for art's sake; here it was, art for the artist's sake. But though it may seem tall talk on the part of the artist who sets up for himself such a standard, in effect it runs the risk often of being but a poor standard.

'But you know', I suggested, 'the main idea of your play is not a pretty one. You take the worst form of murderer, a parricide, and set him up on a pedestal to be worshipped by the simple, honest people of the West. Is this probable?'

'No, it is not; and it does not matter. Was Don Quixote probable? and still it is art.'

'What was it that at all suggested the main idea of the play?' I asked.

'Tis a thing that really happened. I knew a young fellow in the Aran Islands who had killed his father, and the people befriended him and sent him off to America.'

'But did all the girls all make love to him because he had killed his father, and for that only, the sorry looking bedraggled, and altogether repelling figure though he was personally?'

'No. Those girls did not, but mine do.'

'Why do they? What is your idea in making them do it?'

'It is to bring out the humour of the situation. It is a comedy, an extravaganza, made to amuse.' . . . 'Then I am to understand, Mr. Synge, that your play is not meant to represent Irish life. The fact that a story such as depicted by you actually did happen in a modified way is neither here nor there. Life is not made up of isolated occurrences, but of the things that happen day by day. In fact, you had no object whatever in the play except your own art. The plot appealed to your own artistic sense, and for the rest you did not care.'

'Yes', he answered, 'and I don't care a rap how the people take it. I never bother whether my plots are typical Irish or not; but my methods are typical.'

His excitement seemed to go on growing, as if somebody had said something to him during the interval to ruffle him still more. He went on talking to me at a rate which made me glad I was not taking him down in shorthand. . . . I was just able to catch him up at the end, to the effect that the speech used by his characters was the actual speech of the people, and that in art a spade must be called a spade.

'But the complaint is, Mr. Synge, that you call it a bloody shovel. Of course, I am not speaking from personal experience, for I have not heard a word at all from the stage, though I could not possibly be nearer it. And that reminds me, Mr. Synge, what do you propose to do for the rest of the week, in face of what has taken place tonight?'

'We shall go on with the play to the very end, in spite of all', he answered, snapping his fingers, more excited than ever. 'I don't care a rap.'

Dublin Evening Mail, 29 Jan. 1907, p. 2

[Synge gives his version of the interview in a letter to Stephen MacKenna.]

He — the interviewer — got in my way — may the devil bung a cesspool with his skull — and said, 'Do you really think, Mr. Synge, that if a man did this in Mayo, girls would bring him a pullet?' The next time it was, 'Do you think, Mr. Synge, they'd bring him eggs?' I lost my poor temper (God forgive me that I didn't wring his neck) and I said, 'Oh well, if you like, it's impossible, it's extravagance (how's it spelt?). So is Don Quixote!' He hashed up what I had said a great [deal] worse than I expected, but I wrote next day politely backing out of all that was in the interview. That's the whole myth. It isn't quite accurate to say, I think, that the thing is a generalization from a simple case. If the idea had occurred to me I could and would just as readily have written the thing as it stands without the Lynchehaun case or the Aran case. The story — in its *essence* — is probable, given the psychic state of the locality. I used the case afterwards to controvert critics who said it was *impossible*.

Synge, quoted in *Irish Renaissance*, ed. Robin Skelton and David R. Clark (Dublin: Dolmen Press, 1965), p. 75

[Synge responded publicly to the interview in a letter to the *Irish Times*.]

The Playboy of the Western World is not a play with 'a purpose' in the modern sense of the word, but although parts of it are, or are meant to be, extravagant comedy, still a great deal more that is behind it, is perfectly serious when looked at in a certain light. That is often the case, I think, with comedy, and no one is quite sure today whether Shylock and Alceste should be played seriously or not. There are, it may be hinted, several sides to *The Playboy*. 'Pat', I am glad to notice, has seen some of them in his own way. There may still be others if anyone cares to look for them.

Synge, letter to the Editor, *Irish Times*, 31 Jan. 1907, p. 5

['Pat' was Patrick Kenny, who gave the play a favourable review in the *Irish Times*. He saw it as a prophecy 'of the downfall of an Ireland that was exporting its strongest inhabitants and being emotionally and spiritually debilitated by the institution of arranged and loveless marriages.'

The Lynchehaun case and the Aran story cited in Synge's letter to MacKenna are both examples of men wanted for murder being sheltered by local peasants. It is worth noting here the Aran excerpt as it gives a clear indication of the collective psychology that Synge was representing and exploring in the play.]

Another old man, the oldest on the island, is fond of telling me anecdotes — not folk-tales — of things that have happened here in his lifetime. He often tells me about a Connaught man who killed his father with the blow of a spade when he was in a passion, and then fled to this island and threw himself on the mercy of some of the natives with whom he was said to be related. They hid him in a hole — which the old man has shown me — and kept him safe for weeks, though the police came and searched for him, and he could hear their boots grinding on the stones over his head. In spite of a reward which was offered, the island was incorruptible, and after much trouble the man was safely shipped to America.

This impulse to protect the criminal is universal in the west. It seems partly due to the association between justice and the hated English jurisdiction, but more directly to the primitive feeling of these people, who are never criminals yet always capable of crime, that a man will not do wrong unless he is under the influence of a passion which is as irresponsible as a storm on the sea. If a man has killed his father, and is already sick and broken with remorse, they can see no reason why he should be dragged away and killed by the law. Such a man, they say, will be quiet all the rest of his life, and if you suggest that punishment is needed as an example, they ask, 'Would any one kill his father if he was able to help it?'

Synge, *Collected Works, Volume II: Prose*, p. 95

In writing *The Playboy of the Western World*, as in my other plays, I have used very few words that I have not heard among the country people, or spoken in my own childhood before I would read the newspapers. A certain number of the phrases I employ I have heard also among the fishermen of Kerry and Mayo, or from beggars nearer Dublin, and I am glad to acknowledge how much I owe, directly and indirectly, to the folk-imagination of these people. Nearly always when some friendly or angry critic tells me that such or such a phrase could not have been spoken by a peasant, he singles out some expression that I have heard, word for word, from some old woman or child, and the same is true also, to some extent, of the actions and incidents I work with. The central incident of *The Playboy* was suggested by an actual occurrence in the West.

> Synge, programme note for Abbey Theatre production,
> 26 Jan. 1907

[A few weeks after the riots Synge wrote to M. J. Nolan, a young playwright who had sent him an 'interesting and clearheaded' essay on *The Playboy*.]

With a great deal of what you say I am most heartily in agreement — as where you see that I wrote [the play] directly, as a piece of life, without thinking, or caring to think, whether it was a comedy, tragedy, or extravaganza, or whether it would be held to have, or not to have, a purpose — also where you speak very accurately and rightly about Shakespeare's 'mirror'. In the same way, you see — what it seems so impossible to get our Dublin people to see, obvious as it is — that the wildness and, if you will, vices of the Irish peasantry are due, like their extraordinary good points of all kinds, to the *richness* of their nature — a thing that is priceless beyond words.

I fancy when you read the play — or see it performed in more possible conditions — you will find Christy Mahon more interesting than you are inclined to do now. Remember on the first production of a play the most subtle characters always tend to come out less strongly than the simple characters, because those who act the subtle parts can do no more than feel their way till they have acted the whole play a number of times. Whether or not I agree with your final interpretation of the whole play is my secret. I follow Goethe's rule to tell no one what one means in one's writing. I am sure you will agree the rule is a good one.

> Synge, *Collected Works, Volume IV: Plays, Book 2*, p. xxiii

[For a full account of the riots, see Robert Hogan and James Kilroy, *The Abbey Theatre: the Years of Synge, 1905-1909* (Dublin: Dolmen Press 1978), and James Kilroy, *The Playboy Riots* (Dublin: Dolmen Press, 1971).

The Playboy was published by Maunsel in March 1907. George Roberts (of Maunsel, not the Abbey actor) contributed an article in

Shanachie, in which he put the case for Synge to be considered a national dramatist. He saw the play as Synge's 'finest and consequently his most national piece of work: the theme, the setting, the characterization, the rendering through the actual speech of the peasant of all his innate fierceness and brutality, his extravagant humour and wistful tenderness, are all the outcome of a most profound insight into the depths of Gaelic personality. The comedy of a man imagining himself a hero, through his readiness to accept the appreciation of the crowd . . . and his subsequent belief in his own story, has its root in a very common tendency in Ireland. The characters of the drunken publican and his companion, the priest-fearing Shawneen, the widow Quin and old Mahon, contrasted with Pegeen and Christy, make the play an extraordinarily complex and complete representation of Irish life.'

Lady Gregory, early on in the play's composition, had thought that 'there were too many violent oaths, and the play itself was marred by this'. She stood by the play, however, defending it eloquently in an article in *The Arrow*.]

I may say that the play was never acted as it is printed. I know, though I was not present, that it was considerably cut in rehearsal; and after the first public performance, we, the players and I, went through it and struck out any expressions that had given offence, and which were not necessary to the idea. It was so played during its Dublin week, and so it will be played in England. We did nothing, however, to soften or to hide the central idea; we felt that would be an insincerity. This idea may be taken very seriously if taken as a yet to be fulfilled prophecy, and is it not said that every work of art is either a memory or a prophecy? It is a foreshadowing of what will happen if emigration goes on carrying off, year by year, the strongest, the most healthy, the most energetic. . . . The old are always left to us, and the very young, the weakly in body or in mind. Some day it may be not a prophecy but a commonplace that a man coming with a name for strength and daring even in crime may take the mastery of a feeble countryside. Can anyone say that such a tragedy is impossible? And if the idea be a mere fantasy, who is so thinskinned as to take offence? There are some critics, town dwellers for the most part, who would be 'more royalist than the King', and cry out if the Irish peasant is represented with the lack of any virtue — no, if he be even called a peasant.

Lady Gregory, 'An Explanation',
The Arrow, 1 June 1907, p. 5-7

[Miss Horniman arranged for the play to tour England, along with other productions in the repertoire. She thought *The Playboy* to be 'splendid', dismissing 'those silly people who made a noise' as being 'jealous at heart'. When *The Playboy* reached London on 6 June 1907 it was hailed as a masterpiece. The London critics universally praised the performance at the Great Queen Theatre and, according to Hugh Hunt in his history of the Abbey Theatre, Synge became a literary lion overnight. When *The Playboy* was revived in Dublin in 1909 it was warmly received by the audience although the critics remained largely hostile. But the battle was fought again in America when the Abbey Company (described as the Irish Players), accompanied by Lady Gregory, toured major cities on the East Coast. After a favourable start in Boston, the company played in New Haven and Washington without incident. However, in New York there were disturbances and in Philadelphia, following riots, the whole cast was arrested. The warrants were founded on a bill forbidding the performance of 'immoral or indecent plays'. Lady Gregory gives a full account of the tour in *Our Irish Theatre*, p. 97-135. Since these early productions, the play has become part of the Irish classical repertoire. In the following extract from an essay on acting in *The Playboy*, one of Ireland's most respected actors, Cyril Cusack, puts the play in its cultural and theatrical context.]

Having myself, as a child-actor, emerged from the school of melodrama associated with Boucicault and the despised 'stage-Irishman' — which, from Lady Gregory's pronunciamento, the Abbey was pledged to replace with indigenous theatre — I recognized the true theatrical quality of Synge. At the same time, instinctively I felt the necessity of relating the work to reality — as I knew it — and what I then understood as 'reality' was drawn from my observation of Irish speech and character through a touring childhood. So, though I was ignorant of the fact that the dramatist had, as he tells us, composed his dialogue in phrases culled directly from the mouths of the people, without being fully conscious of what I was doing I set out to play in a 'style' compounded of the purely theatrical with a form of naturalism perilously near to being simply representational, two apparently conflicting elements which nevertheless are present and compatible in the work of Synge. Needless to say, there was no great novelty in this, as I was to discover in my subsequent association abroad with many of the first generation Abbey players, of whose work in exile, even through an overlay of commercial theatre, I have had privileged glimpses; I would see that already had been achieved that fine balance of naturalism with the theatrical which was the ideal of Irish acting but which had fallen away, on the one hand into the near vaudevillean method demanded of the Irish actor by foreign commercial managements, and, on the other, into the false convention contrived by some of the later resident disciples of the Abbey tradition, or the pseudo-naturalism, later still, of younger reactionaries. . . .

While allowances were made by the 'traditionalists' for my tentative and more exploratory renderings of Synge in some of the smaller roles — Bartley in *Riders to the Sea*, Owen in *Deirdre of the Sorrows*, even the Tramp in *In the Shadow of the Glen* — when it came for me to play the major roles, of Christy in *The Playboy of the Western World* and Martin Doul in *The Well of the Saints*, murmurings were heard. On the opening night of a revival of the former play, with special settings and costume designs by the artist Sean Keating, the late F. R. Higgins, poet and, at the time, managing director of the theatre, came to my dressing room in a state of indignation: 'No Mayo man ever spoke like that!' he said 'Why would he speak like a Mayo man?' I asked, in some bewilderment. 'Isn't he from Kerry? Doesn't he say . . . 'I'm thinking Satan hasn't many have killed their da in Kerry and in Mayo too?'

Contrarily, the objection was concerned not so much with authenticity of dialect or the character's whereabouts as with the fact that in speaking the speech 'trippingly on the tongue' I had broken with a convention, one which, to my way of thinking, had set a manner of delivery altogether remote from human communication, much as that which, in style of speech, stance, and movement, down to the slightest inflection, the smallest gesture — until revitalized by the modern approach — had mummified the Shakespearean theatre. My heresy hunted out, I pleaded, defending a rather open position, that never had I heard human beings speak so, as this convention demanded, and I disclaimed it as alien to both author and audience. To my relief, the performance was generally accepted as a revival in the literal sense and thenceforward I saw myself as a protagonist of Synge, with a responsibility to communicate his language to the audience as living speech. . . .

The literary group headed by W. B. Yeats and Lady Gregory which controlled, directed, and, indeed, inspired the Abbey Theatre, was of Anglo-Irish Protestant stock. Self-elected cultural leaders, they were properly regarded as such; yet, however idealistically motivated, as interpreters of the native genius they were not in true alignment with it. Synge, of similar stock but apart — the Irishman refound in France, Europeanized — penetrated more deeply into the character of the Gael; and, had he lived longer, with that sensitive ear he might have heard underneath the rural phrases he recorded so assiduously and wove into multi-coloured theatre-designs, the full heart-beat of his people; in revealing more completely and universally its spiritual depths he might indeed have reached the full extent of his own rapidly maturing genius.

From my first playing of Christopher Mahon, which erring on the side of naturalism, I related to myself, I became aware, as the play draws further away from the area of comedy towards its very much less comedic denouement, of some inadequacy, which for many years I attributed to the performance. Only latterly have I formed the opinion, however much it may smack of actor's vanity, that the inadequacy is in the play itself. This becomes evident as, with recurring anti-climax, it moves to its ending.

Christy, moving through a world of make-believe in which his listeners indulge with relish, reaches towards reality and self-discovery; as they accept, so he accepts his story, only here and there touching it with the shadow of positive mendacity; he assumes its central character as an actor identifying himself with the part he plays; but, unfortunately, at the play's ending reality disappears in a balloon-burst of disillusionment and the person of Christopher Mahon suddenly resolves itself into a dew. It is here that, as an actor, I find the part less than satisfying; here, where the playwright in search of himself is confronted with a void which is made the play's resolution. It is liberation, but a false one, of the artist in flight from reality; whom again we are invited to pursue into the mists in *In the Shadow of the Glen* and *The Well of the Saints*. . . . This may be acceptable as a poetic reality within the experience of the playwright but it falls short of universality. . . . Nevertheless, in his craftsmanship, in his sense of theatre, in his imagination and observation, in his desire and striving for identification with reality, Synge is the greatest of the Irish dramatists.

Perhaps my greatest satisfaction in the play was during the first International Theatre Festival in Paris, when, with my company, I presented it at the Sarah Bernhardt Theatre. It was accounted one of the two major contributions to the Festival, the other being Brecht's production of *Mutter Courage*. Here I dare to suggest that the *Playboy* in Paris found its true home and audience. After all, did not the author once live but a few paces from the Odeon?

Cyril Cusack, *Modern Drama*, IV (Dec. 1961), p. 300-4

[The first translation of *Playboy* into French was by Maurice Bourgeois, for the production at the Théâtre de l'Oeuvre on 12 December 1913, directed by Lugné-Poë. Of this, Gerard Leblanc notes: 'The main reaction of the public seems to have been amazement at the paradox of the opening situation, the unchecked flood of language, and, most of all, the rough-and-tumble action in the third act which shocked the audience much more than any mention of female underwear, not an infrequent property on the Paris stage of the time.' ('Synge in France', *A Centenary Tribute to Synge*, ed. S. B. Bushrui, 1979). Critical comments included: 'Audiences either bewildered or bored' and 'shocking for French ears used to finer wit' (*Le Figaro*); 'clumsiness of the author' (*Comoedia*); 'a bitter unpleasant pessimism' and 'how ponderous the irony and how inopportune' (*Le Temps*). The play was mainly criticized for its excesses, its wildness, and its violence: 'The play is too primitive, too spontaneous. . . . It contains too much richness, not enough literal clarity'

(*Comoedia*). Synge might well have been pleased by this observation as he always acknowledged 'the rich joy found only in what is superb and wild in reality'. The poet Guillaume Apollinaire was a lone voice in support of the play. He maintained that 'there has been nothing so realistic and so perfect on stage since Molière or Gogol', and went on to make the following rather pertinent observation: 'In Paris all were indifferent except poets. . . . Poets have always more or less tried to murder their fathers, but it is not an easy thing and looking at the house on the first night I thought: too many fathers, too few sons' (*Soirées de Paris*).

In 1958 the play was transformed into a musical entitled *The Heart's a Wonder*, by Nuala and Mairin O'Farrell, presented at the Gate Theatre, Dublin, on 6 August 1958 in a production by Denis Carey with settings by Micheál MacLiammóir. The airs for their lyrics were taken in the main from Petrie's collection of traditional Irish folk music, the dialogue being an edited version of Synge's original. Most reviewers questioned the value of translating the play into a different form, and when, in September 1958, *The Heart's a Wonder* transferred to the Westminster Theatre in London, Kenneth Tynan, describing the original play as 'a Freudian pastoral', commented that the musical version 'retains most of the text; and the interpolated songs, dressed up with brisk and loyally Syngian lyrics, are all based on traditional songs; if they seem to have only two tunes, one quick and one slow, the fault must lie not with the adaptors but with the poverty of Celtic musical invention.' Tynan thought that 'the play comes through as ironic and eloquent as ever. . . . The end drags on too long but the final line, Pegeen Mike's "I've lost the only playboy of the western world", retains all its mournful inexplicable power' (*The Observer*, 21 Sept. 1958). The play's transference into another medium provided the focus for reviews of Granada's television production in 1958 and the BBC's radio version in 1959. It would seem that the play's rich language lent itself more readily to sound broadcasting.]

In J. M. Synge's *The Playboy of the Western World*, tragi-comedy is stretched to the limit: any production that lays stress on one component at the expense of the other will rob the play of an essential dimension.

English productions tend to err on the side of comedy, crowding the stage with gangs of bibulous drolls, jars of poteen in hand, and prodigally pouring out the golden language as a means of evading any reality in the situation. But Mr. Cliff Owen, in his production of the play last night for Granada, took the opposite course, and knocked a good deal of fun out of the play. Granada's productions have acquired a reputation for austere realism and intimate psychological detail; and it was odd to see Synge receiving such muted inconsequential treatment.

One effect of this approach was to make the language far less enjoyable than usual; although the Irish cast delivered it with irreproachable spontaneity, they threw it out at a pace which left one no time to relish its quality and sometimes obliterated meaning altogether. An equally serious flaw was the undermining of the play's structure. If Christy's boast of having murdered his father raises only mild approval among the villagers, as it did last night, then their savage outcry against his real act of violence as 'a dirty deed' loses its ironic force. Instead of letting tragedy and comedy fight it out on equal terms the production ignored every invitation for comedy, even the sublime anti-climax of Old Mahon's entry on all fours which reprieves Christy from the wrath of the mob.

The Times, 27 Nov. 1958

'On the stage', wrote J. M. Synge, in his preface to *The Playboy of the Western World*, 'one must have reality, and one must have joy.' The production of his play by Mr. Noel Iliff in the BBC Home Service last night as part of the World Theatre series persuaded us of the reality; it is odd how far a local accent and a handful of outlandish idioms can go in persuading us that the riotous glories of Synge's language is the common speech of ordinary men and women. We are driven to profitless speculations about how and to what extent the dramatist transmutes what he hears as common speech. . . . But if the language is Irish, the story is universal — the drudge or dreamer who comes to terms with life through his vices rather than his virtues.

Miss Sheila Manahan and Mr. P. G. Stephens dealt convincingly with Pegeen and Christy, and made their love scenes a thing of great quality, but one feels that the Widow Quin was a slyer person than Miss Peggy Marshal made out. Mr. Jack Cunningham's Old Mahon, vocally bending under the weight of the chip on his shoulder, was touchingly too obsessed with his wrongs to rise to eloquence.

The Times, 19 May 1959

[The Dublin Theatre Festival of 1960 saw one of the most famous performances of the play which shifted the central focus from Christy to Pegeen Mike. The part was played by Siobhán McKenna, an actress with a formidable talent and undoubted charisma, who showed a remarkable affinity with the role and whose knowledge of Gaelic and linguistic agility added yet a further texture to the play's extraordinary verbal richness. The production was directed at the Gaiety by Sheelagh Richards, and transferred to the Piccadilly Theatre, London, in October.]

In appearance she is close to the ideal of Celtic womanhood, which the poets of the Irish renaissance revived in their saga-plays of Deirdre and

Grainne; scarlet hair, tumbling to the waist, elfin-eyed, and with high, slavic cheekbones (though her other features are smaller and more delicate than those of the slavic face). She has perfected for this part a voice which has a unique tonal effect of its own. Certain of these sounds are outside the range of the English phonetic system, taken from Connacht Gaelic (which Miss McKenna speaks) and suggesting the rise and fall of wind and wave which is always in the ears of the people on the Western coast. This is one of the great voices of the stage, enthralling, masterful, married perfectly to the imagery of the lines which Synge himself drew from the Gaelic West. Perhaps early in the play Miss McKenna was a little over-masterful and strident, and her walk, though graceful, too swift for the dimensions of the stage. Still, an enormous performance.

The magnitude of her interpretation sets the play slightly askew. It becomes the tragedy of Pegeen Mike, not the flowering of Christy Mahon. The importance of Synge's play in the European tradition is that, after Cervantes, Mozart, Molière, and Byron, he brought forth a new Don Juan figure — this time a peasant one. Christy Mahon is a shy dreamer, until his famous deed pirouettes him to a pedestal of fame, and he discovers the power of frothy eloquence to conquer a woman's heart. His love language is the flowering of his real personality. The effect of Miss McKenna's playing is such that, when Christy makes his exit in the last act, instead of romping out 'to a romancing lifetime' he slithers out sideways while we wait anxiously for Miss McKenna to intone the famous last line.

Mr. Donal Donelly gave a highly competent performance . . . as Christy Mahon, and made the constellated language of the love scenes seem real, which is the test of all Christy Mahons. Miss Filhume Dunne brought a whiff of womanly pity to the Widow Quin that seemed to bring to the surface something Synge intended, but is seldom portrayed. The production was most satisfactory. One of its distinctive features was that Miss Sheelagh Richards made the actors speak slowly and with great clarity. Thus the outrageously amusing imagery, with which Synge endows almost every character in the play, was easily discerned, and this production seemed to provide more humorous enjoyment than any other performance of *The Playboy* I have seen.

The Times, 16 Sept. 1960

The curtain rose last night on one of those performances that remain, branded in glory, on the memory, when all trivial fond records have been wiped away. . . . Mr. Synge's play is, of course, one of the imperishable masterpieces of European literature. . . . But it is the roaring dam-burst of sheer words that we reel from the theatre remembering. . . . Poetry in these colours, bright as noon-day, beautiful as sunrise, and terrible as an army with banners, has died out of theatrical fashion. It is good to be reminded that there were men like Synge who could pile word on glittering word and stuff the result full of passion and pity and love. . . . It is the playing of Miss Siobhán McKenna as Pegeen that should leave not a seat, not a standing-place, not a nook where a body can be squeezed. Miss McKenna touches her words, and they burst into flame. She tosses her head and the stars dance. She wrings indignation from a look, love from a gasp, and infinite, ravishing beauty from every syllable she utters. It is the kind of performance which comes once, and not again, and nothing short of damnation will suffice for those who miss it.

Bernard Levin, *Daily Express*, 13 Oct. 1960

The first thing that dawned on us as we saw Miss McKenna behind the counter of Michael James's public-house on the wild coast of Mayo in Western Ireland was that she was making sounds of haunting beauty; the second that we could hardly understand a word she was saying. This incomprehension, however, soon passed sufficiently for us to follow what was happening. Miss McKenna properly throughout the evening made no concessions. She had determined to show us that human speech is not bounded by the restrictions of English phonetics: and show us she did. . . . Throughout the entire evening this astonishing flow of beauty, romantic and melancholy as the shadow of a far-off mountain, strange as the taste of nectar, went on, and as our ears became accustomed to it, as our sluggish spirits rose and responded to the challenge, we realized that a whole new world of ravishing speech was being opened to us.

The second thing for which we were not prepared was the performance of Donal Donnelly . . . [which] alone would be sufficient to make this production of Sheelagh Richards's memorable. His Christopher Mahon is young; he rejoices in his follies, his lies, and his imagination; and when in the end their absurdity is exposed he makes us feel as I have not known any of his predecessors do, the crash of the poet's pipes, and the breaking of a spirit which, though ridiculous, is nevertheless real and living. In fact, Mr. Donnelly gives Miss McKenna an unbelievably good run for her money; and it is not until the celebrated last line in the play . . . which she speaks like the echo of an unapproachable, immeasurable sorrow, that Miss McKenna establishes a victory for herself as distinct from that victory for the performance as a whole which was not in doubt after the first five minutes.

Harold Hobson, *Sunday Times*, 16 Oct. 1960.

[This production also toured to Germany, playing in Berlin (West) and Frankfurt. *Playboy* had first been performed in Berlin in 1924, directed by Heinz Hilpert, who apparently over-emphasized its burlesque aspects and turned it into 'a roaring comedy'. Brecht also chose to present *Playboy* at the Schiffbauerdamm Theatre in East Berlin. His assistants, Peter Palitsch and Manfred Wekwerth, directed the play, according to *The Times* reviewer, 'in a setting so realistically Irish that not even the turf fire on the open hearth nor the white bawneen trousers of the Playboy are overlooked.' He continues: 'One of the principles of Brecht's production methods is 'to play the story'. Here it is not Synge's story that is played, but another, with a different purpose. Its content is still psychologically less satisfying, though it may be didactically more useful. However, Manfred Wekwerth is proud to have produced the play as a comedy' (*The Times*, 21 August 1956).

In January 1971 the play was performed by the prestigious Repertory Theatre of the Lincoln Center in New York in a production directed by John Hirsch. Jack Kroll thought the actors played 'to a better level than their usual, without reaching the true heights', going on to make some perceptive comments about the nature and function of the play's language.]

Synge's language is the earthy and divine rant of creatures who have to fabricate a glory to counteract the onerous reality of their lives. The beautiful blarney is an index of the freedom of their spirits and the transvaluing power of art, which in this sense belongs to everyone. Christy's father thinks of his son as a 'fool', but Pegeen Mike loves him for the spirit which can make him give her a vision of their love 'making mighty kisses with our wetted mouths, or gaming in a gap of sunshine, with yourself stretched back into your necklace, in the flowers of the earth'.

Jack Kroll, *Newsweek*, 18 Jan. 1971

[*The Playboy* was given a notable revival by the National Theatre, London, first at the Old Vic in October 1975 and then in a transfer to the new building on the South Bank in January 1976. Christy Mahon was played by Stephen Rea, a young Irish actor who was to become one of the most interesting of his generation. When asked in an interview if the prospect of playing Christy alarmed him, he replied: 'Very much: this is after all *the* Irish part: it's like working with Irish history, and when people come into the theatre the chances are they'll already know the play, so they'll be looking that much more carefully at the performances. I don't like thinking of myself as an exclusively Irish actor, I'd rather just be an actor, but with a part like Christy you simply have to let the national identity take over' (*Times Saturday Review*, 1 Nov. 1975). He was to add: 'It's a wonderful play and a wonderful part. All Irish actors of my type aspire to it. It's the Irishman's Hamlet.'

The play was directed by Bill Bryden, who was aware that it is not only peculiarly Irish but also transcends its national boundaries: 'You must remember that when we open in London it's not to an Irish audience, though many Irish born will certainly come to see it. You won't have the same sense of identification on the part of the people who sit there in their seats and look and listen. In Ireland, this play is part of people's tradition, and leaving the famous riots at its first performance aside, you will always have a reaction to the fact that it is deeply critical of the Irish character. The way people created a hero because they wanted one, and then brought him down because that's what they do. Fine, that's a good summary of what the play is about, but it is not specifically Irish and not specifically anti-Irish. It's the same as saying that John Osborne wrote a vocationally anti-English play when he wrote *Look Back in Anger*. I don't think he did. Jimmy Porter could have been any nationality. He reflected a mood of that time, but the play had its roots in its own country, it spread everywhere.'

The reviews were mostly positive. Charles Lewson of *The Times* thought it was 'an evening in which to be a little drunk and a little in love'. B. A. Young in the *Financial Times* did not 'believe the Abbey Theatre at its best could have excelled this production of Synge's masterpiece', and Peter Lewis found the smell of the peat fire in the white-washed cottage 'very beguiling'. Michael Billington, however, added a dissenting voice in *The Guardian*, commenting that if the National Theatre 'felt it time to make a genuflection to Irish drama, why didn't they look to a troubled topical unflakeable masterpiece like *The Plough and the Stars*' (Bill Bryden did in fact direct a production of O'Casey's play at the National a few years later). The following reviews give a range of critical opinion, including an interesting piece by John Barber on Synge's dialogue. The last review by Irving Wardle shows how the transfer to the open stage of the Olivier Theatre freed the production visually. He also mentions the Chieftains, the celebrated Irish folk band which supplied all the musical accompaniment, adding a further note of authenticity to the performance.]

The first casualty of Mr. Bryden's approach . . . was the sense of landscape, the wild isolation of the Mayo coast. The cottage might have been an authentic reconstruction, but the people who dropped in and out might have done so from almost any village green. This had consequences for the play, because when the Playboy leaves, a desperate isolation should descend upon Pegeen. Where in this desert can she find another like him, who is brave enough not to murder, but to control, his father? Without a surrounding desert, Susan Fleetwood was like any other girl who has lost the one she fancies.

The lack of Mayo wildness also puts a new perspective on the language, which becomes vague and Irish Literary, instead of emerging from the surrounding shadows and understandable superstitions. It prevents the feeling of enclosure to the wooing scenes and turns the characters into Irish stock types. This meant that the struggle to hang Christy became a clumsy farce, and that there was no sudden shock of recognition when the myth became reality, when the 'gallows story' is revealed as 'a dirty deed'.

John Elsom, *The Listener*, 6 Nov. 1975

The dialogue, as Synge said, is 'fully flavoured as a nut or apple' and an excellent company savours all its crackle and juice. The play's central situation is full of comic potential. . . . But underneath this lyrical, oedipal comedy, Synge writes not only of the desolation of Ireland — a lonely land inhabited only by the old and the timid young — but also, through the person of the playboy, Christy, plots the gradual liberation of an individual from a stereotype forced upon him and the freeing of his imagination so that his speech soars as he grows in confidence at his own poetic powers.

Stephen Rea conveys this beautifully, growing from a hunched and sullen figure to strutting manhood. As Pegeen Mike, the girl who loves him, Susan Fleetwood reveals the tenderness that lies under the apparent bluster but tends to stiffen in her romantic moments. There is excellent support from such actors as Liam Redmond, J. G. Devlin, P. G. Stephens, and Eddie Byrne.

Margaret Whiting is acidly amusing as Widow Quin, although she plays the part with the clipped intonation and sexual innuendo of Mae West. When Christy begs her to help him with Pegeen and says that he'll pray for her so that at death she may come easily 'to the footstool of the Virgin's son', her reaction — a spasm of distaste at the word 'virgin' — is wonderfully funny. The production as a whole gave me more pleasure and joy than anything I have seen this year.

International Herald Tribune, 12 Nov. 1975

In Bill Bryden's beautiful production . . . the comic irony of the story spreads a glow of happiness, while at the same time its sadness troubles the heart — the sadness of lives so stagnant they can be uplifted by a pack of lies. Its effect is due to its language. As always in the theatre, once we are persuaded to accept a vivid new way of talking, it can hurt and harry us. It can also make us laugh. Much of Synge's comedy arises from his self-parody of a sometimes grotesquely inflated idiom. *Under Milk Wood* turned exactly the same trick.

Nicholas Grene, an author and scholar who lived most of his life in Synge country, maintains . . . that Synge's dialect is faked. He *based* it on authentic speech, but added an artificial colouration aimed at a middle-class urban audience to whom peasant life was unfamiliar and romantic — as, to a degree, it was to Synge. . . . When he came to invent dialogue, he began with primitive Irish speech — and then touched it up to make it more Irish. A simple example: the peasant who had actually said 'Are you wanting money?' turns up in Synge saying: 'Is it gold you might be wanting?' To devise a speech suitable for his drama, he spent hours at his desk, refining and cooking. He avoided obvious Irishisms. The constructions he favoured he used frequently; those he avoided he avoided completely. In this way a limited number of constructions were readily comprehensible to a non-Irish audience.

A favourite device, taken straight from the Irish, was the use of 'and' where we would prefer a subordinate clause: 'Was there anyone on the last bit of the road, stranger, and you coming from Aughrim?' Another is the continuous present: it is always 'I'm thinking' or 'I'm saying', never 'I think' or 'I say'. His humour is unsleeping: 'The Lord protect us from the saints of God!' Many sentences are long, but the concentration can be intense. Try rewriting more briefly: 'Which way would I live and I an old woman if I didn't marry?' . . . The dialogue is a studied artefact exploited for poetic and dramatic purposes. You could say the same of Racine. The effect does not depend on the representation of simple people speaking realistic 'poetic' dialect, though Synge took pains to pretend everything he wrote was authentic. On the contrary, it depends on the colour and the texture of a deliberately artificial language, carefully controlled.

As a result, our minds are engaged by the medium of language itself, just as at the opera we are enmeshed by the tunes and harmonies. In making this so brilliantly clear, Dr. Grene has demolished Synge the too-Irish warbler of native wood-notes wild, and unveiled in his place an exquisite artist.

John Barber, *Daily Telegraph*, 19 Jan. 1976

Geoffrey Scott's shebeen from floor to chimneystack is slewed over the front of the stage angled towards the left of the house. Through the door you see the cobbled yard from which Christy stumbles in out of the night; behind that a dry stone wall, leading the eye up to a level above the house where the red petticoats come racing over the hill and drinkers get a fine view of the village sports; and behind that, inky blackness. The cold of the heath is there as well as the warmth of the hearth. And as the Chieftains' barbaric reel dies down with the house lights, there is Pegeen Mike flat on her stomach dreamily compiling her trousseau.

The Playboy is a piece about what the Kerry dramatist George Fitzmaurice called the 'wicked old children' of the west of Ireland. It is still a weird, harsh story that resists easy cultural assimilation much more stoutly than O'Casey. And the one decision that runs through every part of the production, set, music, and performances, is the refusal to perform the usual nosedive into Syngean lyricism.

77

Those sing-song cadences have put off many a potential convert to this author. Here you are aware of them mainly as a channel carrying a marvellous flow of images; and the cast ride them instead of being engulfed. Miss Fleetwood, for instance, presents a Pegeen I have never seen before: a girl who knows her rough tongue is her worst enemy and who welcomes Christy as someone who can still it. The situation is as much concerned with her transformation as with his: and that comes over as clearly when she is pummelling his bed and slinging his shoes across the floor as when she melts under his cascade of fine talk.

Stephen Rea's Christy, a scarecrow even in his borrowed best clothes and triumphant sporting kit, likewise illuminates every stage of shedding the past and taking on a new identity. Synge's language preserves his dignity, but you can feel the cold in his bones, the loneliness, and the growing rage. The production paves every step for his lightning transformation from false heroics into the real thing.

Angela Galbraith . . . as the Widow Quin challenges Pegeen on her own ground of youth and good looks; but, however unbalancing the effect, it is hard to regret so ironically seductive a performance or, for that matter, Jim Norton's departure from Synge's 'fat and fair' young Sean who appears as an abject, rabbity underling, who tries to attract his fiancee's attention by pulling on her like a bell-rope. A splendid show.

Irving Wardle, *The Times*, 8 Oct. 1976

[In the summer of 1982 the Druid Theatre in Galway on the West Coast of Ireland, founded by Garry Hynes (later Artistic Director of the Abbey Theatre in Dublin), presented what was to become the most famous contemporary interpretation of the play. The production played at the Edinburgh International Festival, the Dublin Theatre Festival, toured the Aran Islands, and was eventually seen at the Donmar Warehouse in London, where it was filmed for transmission by Channel Four on 17 March 1986.]

The quaint set . . . at once captivating and intriguing . . . with meticulous detail recreates at once for us the required atmosphere: the thatched cottage from the rafters of which hang the bacon and the fishing nets, the old turf fire complete with all the trappings, the old-fashioned pub with its heaped-up piles of crocks and smokey fires; it is all there.

The production by Garry Hynes is *The Playboy* at its best, full of colour so characteristic of Synge. It has all the lilt and flow of the poetic language right through, even as Pegeen cries 'there's a great gap between a gallant story and a dirty deed'; it never sags; the ferocity of the language sweeps on as do the waves of the shore and the characters act and react with great intensity. It is an exciting production.

An tSuir-Aibhle, *Galway Advertiser*, 19 Aug. 1982

Druid, a theatre group from Galway city, catch a flavour of the west of Ireland (Mayo) as authentic as the effects of too much poteen. . . . The humour burbles, the sly glad-eye of the playwright is caught by Maeliosa Stafford in the title role. A prim Shawneen by Sean Mcginley sets an authentic tone at the start. A clatter of syllables by Marie Mullen as the Widow Quin keeps the momentum going and counterpoints perfectly the reeling drunken cumming of the Playboy's father as played by Mick Lally.

However, pride of all is Brid Brennan as Pegeen Mike, itching for relief from tedium and raring to go. . . . One only hopes the furniture will last the pace as she woodpeckers her resentment through a fantastic fight scene in the third act.

Hayden Murphy, *The Scotsman*, 2 Sept. 1982

The Druid Theatre Company's . . . production, under Garry Hynes's direction, which opened at the Olympia Theatre last night in the Dublin Theatre Festival, is simply the best I have ever seen. It has kept the comedy without which Synge's drama would be devoid of sympathy. Yet it has drawn as clearly and as cruelly as might once have provoked riots the narrow-eyed, smallminded peasant society in which this realistic drama can only be fully credible.

Pegeen starts out scraping the left-overs into the bin. Christy, after a few minutes' acquaintance, is picking his dirty feet. The Widow Quin has a seedy sexuality which makes her a convincing threat to Pegeen's hatchet-faced, thin-lipped determination. And Christy, having barely lifted an eyelash to any woman, cannot know the harridan Pegeen most assuredly is. His bullet-headed stupidity is proof against the more romantic silliness to which this play, in previous productions, has been most prone to fall. He recognizes only the authority in the woman — an authority which he has barely laid by striking his father a blow with a loy. . . .

David Nowlan, *Irish Times*, 28 Sept. 1982

Ms. Hynes's production knows when to take its time. The opening finds Pegeen delicately, painfully, stamping an envelope, carefully writing the order for provisions to the wholesaler with the occasional ruefully wondering look into space, resigned but not yet hopeless. The fugitive Christy's entrance takes him tottering tentatively across the bar to the breathless silence of the bystanders. The realism extends to the girls' mud-encrusted feet and dirty hands. The tragedy of a poet wasted, a woman blazingly out of place, is movingly brought out. Brid Brennan's Pegeen is short-fused. It takes little to get her nagging, and her tirades end in exasperated near-weeping. Maeliosa Stafford plays Christy as consistently sweet-natured. His touch of the poet, all 'savagery and fine

79

words', is subjected to a vigorous battering from his alleged victim, Old Mahon, bloody and tramp-like in Mick Lally's ferociously robust reading. The almost physical transformation of Ms. Brennan's broad firm-boned face by radiant pride as Christy carries off the sporting honours is deeply moving. The central relationship is ably supported by Marie Mullen's cheerful Widow Quin, and Sean Mcginley's Keogh, both free of exaggeration.

Martin Hoyle, *Financial Times*, 28 Feb. 1985

J. M. Synge's claims for realism, or 'reality', on behalf of his play have never cut serious ice outside the Celtic twilight. It is not that his characters are all credulous, genial, stupid, and brutish, but that they are those things in more or less the same way and almost to the same degree. As in straight farce, character is reduced to elementals, an excuse for boisterous antagonism. Once the black comedy is brought to the fore, the problem of the fantastical language that the young Brendan Behan so delighted in mocking ceases to be a problem at all: that is just the way they speak and this is just the way they act.

The intimacy of the Warehouse's layout does the play the favour of reducing its parade of grotesques to a manageable roomful of quare fellows with whom we become, for the duration of the piece, convivial. Flaherty's bar is a rough shebeen with a stable door. The Sacred Heart on the chimney breast seems to be raising His eyes less in devotion than in despair at the unholy shenanigans taking place beneath Him.

From his first entrance as a wild-eyed vagrant, Maeliosa Stafford makes an engagingly deranged Playboy, a slack-lipped simpleton who discovers a thing or two about imposing on other simpletons. Brid Brennan's Pegeen Mike could hardly be more bitter in her scornful moments but could be considerably more winsome in her tender ones; it is hard to believe that she admires the Playboy for any other reason than that the other females do too. But then, as Joyce observed, 'these characters only exist on the Abbey stage'. To say that now they only exist on the Warehouse stage is intended as a compliment to this production.

Martin Cropper, *The Times*, 28 Feb. 1985

[The most recent productions of *The Playboy* in Britain were at the West Yorkshire Playhouse, directed by Jude Kelly (Feb. 1991), and the Glasgow Citizens' Theatre, directed by Giles Havergal (Sept. 1991). The Abbey's most recent production was in 1988, and Fintan O'Toole's review suggests that it was only partially successful in freeing the play from its traditional 'naturalistic' performance style.]

John Millington Synge was a fabulous inventor, and few of the inventions were more fabulous than the notion that he got much of his dialogue, as he explained in the preface to *The Playboy of the Western World* 'from a chink in the floor that let me hear what was being said by the servant girls in the kitchen'. The point was partly a reasonable one — that his fantastic speech bore a real relationship to the language of ordinary people — but it was also partly a very clever pre-emptive strike against his enemies. What better way to confound those who attacked *The Playboy* as an alien caricature of the Irish peasantry than present yourself as merely the recorder of the plain people's imagination?

It was a smart move in the short term, but in the long term it encouraged the view that the only way to defend *The Playboy* was to present it as a naturalistic play, a slice of peasant life. For a play that is so obviously, in Synge's phrase, 'superb and wild', so poetic and symbolic a comedy, this is a remarkable misunderstanding.

It is *The Playboy*'s very distance from daily life, its magnificent language that owes as much to Shakespeare and the King James Bible as to the speech of the Aran Islands, that makes it so realistic in the deeper sense, so closely connected to the reality of Irish history and Irish life. *The Playboy* is for us a kind of myth, an oblique story which at the same time sends out myriad resonances; the change from arranged, tribal marriages (Shawn Keogh whom Pegeen ditches for the Playboy is her second cousin) to romantic sexuality; the ambivalence towards violence in our culture; the curious relationship between language and reality. It remains a magnificent play, but for all sorts of reasons other than naturalistic fidelity to life as it was in the Mayo of Synge's time.

To judge from Noel Sheridan's fine set, you would think that Vincent Dowling was to give us a far from naturalistic interpretation of the play at the Abbey. The set is highly stylized, with the minimum of naturalistic detail, huge painted backdrops and the interior setting of Michael James Flaherty's shebeen opened out to the surrounding darkness in an intelligent and imaginative step that gives Dowling's staging most of its strengths. The opening minutes, in particular, gain an impressive sense of menace, making sense of Pegeen's fear of being left alone in the house, from the starkness of the setting. Later on, too, Dowling uses the openness of the set to give a fluidity of movement to his production . . . which is in most respects capably orthodox rather than innovative or imaginative. Its most important deficiency is its failure to suggest any hint of the sexual tension that should run through the play like a live wire. Barry Lynch's Kerry Playboy is very impressive in itself, and Ger Ryan's Pegeen is subdued but with a convincing streak of ferocity. There is virtually no connection between them, however, no spark of attraction to give substance to their love-talk. He is the boy in the bubble, she the girl in the glass case.

Similarly, Nuala Hayes's Widow Quin, while rightly young, vibrant, and attractive, has nothing of that character's hunger, the peculiar mixture of sexual and material lust that makes her so memorable. Other actors, most notably Niall O'Brien's splendidly shambolic Old Mahon, do very well, but at times some are forced to slip into an irritatingly inappropriate slapstick. It all makes for a crisp, highly competent production, that does not venture beyond surfaces or risk adventures.

Fintan O'Toole, *Sunday Tribune*, 10 Apr. 1988

[The programme to this production contained a perceptive note which put the first production of the play into its historical perspective.]

Let us not look down too haughtily on those playgoers and critics who reacted with such fury to the original production of *The Playboy of the Western World* at the Abbey Theatre eighty-one years ago. Some were outraged by 'the coarse and blasphemous language'. A few were shocked — and we should probably assume their sincerity — by the public naming, in mixed company, of a woman's undergarment. But the indignation was deepest among those who perceived the play as 'un-Irish'.

Audiences at the time were justifiably touchy about the popular image of the stage-Irishman — a drinking, roaring, swearing, fighting, red-necked broth of a boy. The depiction of such figures by English touring companies was offensive enough, but the presentation of apparently viler caricatures in what purported to be an Irish National Theatre was the last straw. The worst specimen of stage Irishman of the past is a refined, acceptable fellow compared with that imagined by Mr. Synge. 'It is not too much to say that no traducer of the Irish people ever presented a more sordid, squalid, and repulsive picture of Irish life and character.' To make matters worse, the people depicted in the play were without exception immoral, the men drunken and feckless, the women covetous and immodest. 'One looks in vain for a glimmer of Christianity in the acts and utterances of the characters.'

To many in the audience (or not), and especially to those with an understandably heightened consciousness of shoneenism, this 'calumny gone raving mad' merely confirmed what they had suspected all along, that the Irishness of Yeats and Synge and their literary and artistic cronies was not more than skin-deep. When Yeats brought in 'English' police to quell vociferous disturbances in the theatre, he merely jumped out of the Catholic frying-pan into the Nationalist fire.

Why, then, do we not find the play offensive today? True, our norms of 'coarseness' have changed, we have grown self-confident enough to spend a little less time looking over our shoulders, and few of us now blush at the word 'shift'. But are we really not at all upset to see young women throwing themselves at a man because they believe he has slain his father, then spurning him when they discover he failed to finish the job properly? Are we really amused by the spectacle of an opportunist shebeen-owner entrusting his daughter overnight to the care of a fugitive patricide? Do we really think a girl would achieve greater fulfilment married to a lyrical liar than to a law-abiding farmer? Is that how we imagine Ireland? Or Europe? Or the world?

Like every complex work, *The Playboy* does not easily yield up its full meaning. Unlike a photograph, its focus is not definitively fixed. If we see the play only as a social documentary, its wild irony becomes a disruptive intrusion. If we see it only as peasant comedy, its essential harshness is obscured.

How, then, should we view it? Perhaps a few words from the author may help us to hold our minds open: 'I wrote *The Playboy* directly, without thinking, or caring to think, whether it was comedy, tragedy, or extravaganza, or whether it would be held to have, or not to have, a purpose.' . . . And also a few words from his defender W. B. Yeats: 'A dramatist is not an historian.'

Sean Page, programme for Abbey Theatre production, 1988

Deirdre of the Sorrows

Written: 1907-09.

First production: Irish Players, Abbey Theatre, Dublin, 13 Jan. 1910 (dir. Maire O'Neill; des. Charles Riketts (costumes) and Robert Gregory (sets); with Sara Allgood as Lavarcham, Arthur Sinclair as Conchubar, Sydney J. Morgan as Fergus, and Maire O'Neill as Deirdre).

Published: limited editions, Churchtown, Dublin: Cuala Press, 1910, and New York: John Quinn, 1910; in *The Works of J. M. Synge, Volume II* (Dublin: Maunsel, 1910); *Collected Works, Volume IV: Plays, Book 2* (Oxford University Press, 1968); *Complete Plays* (London: Methuen, 1981); *Plays, Poems, and Prose* (London: Dent, 1992).

Conchubar, an aged High King of Ulster set his heart on Deirdre, whom he had reared, and sought to make her his Queen. But she, delighting in the wild freedom of the woods and mountains, responded not to his earnest entreaties; and fled with a lover somewhat of her own age, Naisi, to Alban, where they both lived for seven years in a tent, accompanied by Naisi's two brothers, Amule and Ordan. Through the intervention of Fergus, another Irish monarch, and an old woman Lavarcham, who had apparently acted in the capacity of nurse to Deirdre, they were all induced to return, with the result that Naisi and his brothers were slain by Conchubar's retainers, and Deirdre, becoming demented under the burden of her sorrow, after much heart-rendering lamentation falls lifeless ultimately across their open grave, the amorous Conchubar being led away from the scene a doddering old imbecile.

The only spark of brightness or humour introduced was contributed by the grotesque antics of a fool named Owen, a character of which much might probably have been made had it been properly developed and utilized. On the whole, however, the play was favourably received, and the scenery, especially that of the second act, was greatly admired.

The Irish Independent, 14 Jan. 1910

[In a letter written on 12 September 1907 to Frederick J. Gregg, an Irish-American journalist and an admirer of his work, Synge indicated his intention to write 'a play on Deirdre — it would be amusing to compare it with Yeats and Russell (AE) — but I am a little afraid that the "Saga" people might loosen my grip on reality.' To Molly Allgood he wrote on December 1906: 'My next play must be quite different from [*Playboy*]. I want you to act in it.' Nearly a year later, on 9 November 1907, he told her: 'I have been working at *Deirdre* till my head is going round. I was too taken up with her yesterday to write to you — I got her into such a mess as I think I'd have put her into the fire, only that I want to write a part for *you*, so you mustn't be jealous of her. Since yesterday I have pulled two acts into one, so that, if I can work it, the play will have three acts instead of four, and that has of course given me many problems to think out. As it is, I am not sure that the plan I have is a good one. Ideas seem admirable when they occur to you, and then they get so doubtful when you have thought over them for a while.' And later the same day: 'I am writing myself sick with *Deirdre* or whatever you call it. It is a very anxious job. I don't want to make a failure.' And two days later: 'I did a good deal of work on *Deirdre,* not on the MS, but just notes for a new scene in it.' Then on 27 November: 'My dear child, I'm at my wits end to know what to do — I'm squirming and thrilling and quivering with the excitement of writing *Deirdre* and I *daren't* break the thread of composition by going out to look for digs and moving into them at the moment. . . . Let me get *Deirdre* out of danger — she may be safe in a week — then marriage in God's name.' And on 1 December; 'I've finished the [eighth] version or rewriting of Act III yesterday. It goes all through — the Act III I mean — but it wants a good deal of strengthening, of making personal, still before it will satisfy me.'

Into the New Year, on 7 January, he wrote to Molly with details of his revisions to the first act, the last draft of which is dated 7 March

1908: then, on 3 April, Synge went into hospital and had an operation on 4 May. He was not well enough to resume work on the play until August. He wrote to Molly on 24 August: 'I've decided to cut off the second act — you remember Jesus Christ says if the second act offend thee pluck it out; but I forget you're a heathen, and there's no use quoting Holy Scriptures to you.' On 29 August he wrote to Lady Gregory: 'I have been fiddling with *Deirdre* a little. I think I'll have to cut it down to two longish acts. The middle act in Scotland is impossible.' Impeded again by ill health and the death of his mother, he did not return to work on the play until November. On 22 December he wrote to Molly: 'I've pretty nearly gone on to the end of *Deirdre* and cut it down a little. It is a delicate work — a scene is so easily spoiled. I am anxious to hear you read it to me.'

On 3 January 1909 he told Lady Gregory: 'I have done a great deal to *Deirdre* since I saw you — chiefly in the way of strengthening motives and recasting the general scenario — but there is still a good deal to be done with the dialogue, and some scenes in the first act must be re-written to make them fit in with the new parts I have added. I only work a little every day as I suffer more than I like with indigestion and general uneasiness inside — I hope it is only because I haven't quite got over the shock of the operation — the doctors are vague and don't say much that is definite.' A month later he was admitted to hospital and died on 24 March. He had scribbled on the back of a fragment of Deirdre's keen over the grave of Naisi, 'Unfinished play of *Deirdre*, can be sent if desired to Mr. W. B. Yeats'.

Lady Gregory and Molly Allgood worked on the manuscript during the summer of 1909. It was a mammoth task to create order and form from the material, given the number of revisions and typescript pages. According to Ann Saddlemyer, editor of the plays in the *Collected Works*, Molly and Lady Gregory were ignorant of the additional notebook material. She comments: 'According to Yeats, the editors finally decided to produce the play without any additional material or alterations, and the same assemblage of manuscripts was used by the Cuala Press for their edition of April 1910. Although notes to the present edition suggest that alterations have been made by an unknown hand, especially to Deirdre's final speeches, it is conceivable that these were written in by Molly during Synge's final frantic revisions. The only definite allocations that can be made to others occur in minor stage directions, and here again they were probably determined by Molly, who directed the first production' (*Collected Works, Volume III: Plays, Book 2*, p. xxvii-xxx). In a programme note for the first production at the Abbey in January 1910, Synge's intention to develop the character of Owen is made clear.]

Mr. Synge began writing this play about two years before his death, but it was often put aside because of illness, and was left at the last unfinished. He had brought in a new character, Owen, and had meant to make more use of him, and he would have enriched and elaborated the dialogue, working it over and over again according to his custom. We are giving it as he left it, putting in not more than a half-dozen words and taking out here and there a sentence that did not explain itself.

Programme note, Abbey Theatre production, 13 Jan. 1910

[Maire O'Neill assembled a strong cast which included her sister Sara Allgood, Arthur Sinclair, and Sydney Morgan. Joseph Holloway's reaction was fairly typical of a large section of the audience, and critical comment was mixed.]

His idea seems to have been to wrest the legend from its exalted plane and breathe the common places of everyday life into it — in fact, to vulgarize the beautiful legend. That he succeeded in doing this is only too true. The characters of Lavarcham . . . of Owen, a half-witted servant, and of an old woman might have stepped out of any of his latter-day peasant plays; the muck of muck was in their speech. As a stage play, I fear Synge's *Deirdre of the Sorrows* is of little worth. Up to a certain point, the last act is dramatic, but there it is allowed to fizzle out drearily in ineffective anti-climaxes, and the final curtain comes as a relief to all in front, even to Synge's most ardent worshippers. . . . When the play was over and done, Seamus O'Sullivan said, as many of us chattered in the vestibule, that 'There was nothing incomplete about it. The people in the play were human beings at all events and not merely inanimate Kings and Queens!' I grant that the loftiness of the theme was trailed in the mud if that's what he meant by 'human beings', but the treatment took the grandeur and poetry out of the tale. . . . All seemed afraid to express themselves freely or candidly on the play when it was over, but that the general impression was not favourable could easily be felt. Were the play an undoubted success, nothing could keep back the hymns of praise. It is only when failure is close at hand that silence holds thoughts in check.

Joseph Holloway's Abbey Theatre, p. 133-4

The sorrowful story of Deirdre has given more inspiration to our playwrights than any other of the Irish tales. . . . It was well known that the late Mr. J. M. Synge had been working at it before his death. The announcement that the result would be given at the Abbey was received with much interest. It met with an enthusiastic reception at its first production on the Thursday night of last week.

The dialogue undoubtedly would have been enriched and elaborated had the writer been able to complete it. It bears the impress of his individuality, poetic with the Nature touches so characteristic of his work. Idiomatic and vigorous on occasion, it was played almost as he left it. It is a fine piece of dramatic work, and exhibits Synge's genius in a new light.

It is a human Deirdre Mr. Synge has given us. The play diverges from the familiar tradition in some respects. A new character, Owen, is introduced. Lavarcham, the nurse, also appears in all three acts. . . . Miss Maire O'Neill was a distinct success as Deirdre. The more one sees of Miss O'Neill's playing the more one is convinced that she possesses a true artistic temperament. Her grit was restrained but forceful. As the young girl her passion was poetic and touching. Hers was the chief part in the tragedy; hers the principal triumph of the evening. Miss Sara Allgood was Lavarcham. The nurse undoubtedly was more the duchess than the common woman. Some of the language put in her mouth is not of the heroic order. It may be said that Miss Allgood rendered the part much as the author conceived it.

Firin, *The Irish Times*, 14 Jan. 1910

The truth is that, by some curious process . . . Synge arrived at a delicate appreciation of the colour and mystery of life without gaining any knowledge of the light which gave birth to the colour, or of the spirit lurking behind the mystery. Lacking informative power, his art had no health in it, could only deal with the beauty of externals, of decay. Roses he grew in abundance but all are rooted in a charnel house.

W. J. Lawrence, *The Stage*, 20 Jan. 1910

[Robert Hogan in *The Abbey Theatre: the Rise of the Realists, 1910-1915*, offers the following explanation for this rather muffled response: 'Most accounts report that the reaction to the play was enthusiastic, but others report that the entire production was depressing and even soporific. The reasons for this discrepency were probably these: the ill-feeling about Synge's earlier work was still rawly evident, but it was counterbalanced by the sobering fact that the playwright was dead, and even that his death may have been hastened by the 1907 riots. In any event *Deirdre* did not offer much to fight about. If its psychology was thought to be a demeaningly modern treatment of the legend, its production by Yeats and Maire O'Neill was utterly, even a little boringly, reverent' (p. 19). The English critics were more objective and in some cases condemnatory when the Abbey Players performed *Deirdre* in London in the summer of 1910.]

Deirdre of the Sorrows moves haltingly upon the borderland between intention and achievement, in a dramatic half-world of blurred outlines. It was clearly meant to be a great tragedy, but it is not a great tragedy, and if the rewriting of it was to have been concerned, as Mr. Yeats suggests, mainly with the enrichment and elaboration of its dialogue, it would still have failed. Embroidery of a phrase is a good servant but a poor master. It can easily strangle drama.

Ashley Dukes, *The New Age,* 16 June 1910

The tragedy impresses by its profound pathos and by the simplicity of a phraseology rich in suggestiveness. . . . The play is permeated with that weird sense of mysticism and of fatalism so peculiarly the attribute of the Celtic nature. Crude it is in many respects, but any imperfections it possesses are simply atoned for by the delicacy and beauty of the treatment. Of the hapless heroine, Miss Maire O'Neill gives a wonderfully womanly and tender recount. Her voice is exquisitely sympathetic, and her powers of emotion considerable.

The Daily Telegraph, 31 May 1910

One cannot judge this play by ordinary canons: some will find it dull, unconvincing, but all who have sense of the beauty of words and rhythm will feel the touch of the true poet. It is extraordinarily simple, yet how sensitive and exquisite in its tone modulations, its choice of words, its harmony of movement, like music! Miss Maire O'Neill is always a joy. Her Deirdre is a thing of beauty — the woman so calm, so dark, so soft, so full of soul and femininity, like a Southern Spaniard, and her diction so clear, so resonant, so delicate and musical. It is a pleasure to see her walk, erect, supple, natural, like a woman of the soil, accustomed to carrying a pitcher on her head. She is a thing to see . . . the beauty of Synge's language and the beauty of being and expression of Miss O'Neill made an evening of charm and delight.

A. H., *The Daily Mail,* 31 May 1910

[The American reaction to two productions, ten years apart, is far more positive and laudatory.]

Deirdre is the Irish tale of a lonely maiden who runs away from the ageing King who wants to marry her and takes refuge with the idyllic youth she loves on a wooded island off the coast. Like most Irish legends, this one should not be described, because it is compounded of wonder, innocence, and peat smoke. But Synge was the man who could make the English language dance with loveliness and rapture. Poet of nature, he knew the sounds and savours of the outdoors, the music of wind and rain, and the simple comfort of shelter in a storm. He poured all his love of the greenness of Ireland into this literary and dramatic incantation with its sadness and tenderness and its sorrow over the cruelty of men. . . .

Despite obvious misperfections in the performance, this playgoer is grateful to the Abbey Workshop for mounting a glorious drama under the direction of a man who appreciates it. . . . *Deirdre of the Sorrows* is a difficult play to act. But it is the work of a master of the English language. Even an indifferent performance puts us in debt to Synge's personal modesty and lyric genius.

Brooks Atkinson, *New York Times*, 15 Dec. 1949

It is all too clear why John Millington Synge's *Deirdre of the Sorrows* is so rarely seen in this country. It is a lyrical masterpiece that makes almost impossible demands on the actors. This is particularly true of the two lovers, Deirdre and Naisi, who must combine youth and beauty with the ability to speak Irish poetry liltingly and to rise to the heights of classical tragedy. Such a combination is hard to come by, even on Broadway.

The off-Broadway troupe that staged the play at the Gate Theatre last evening struggles valiantly with the Irish idiom and spirit, and often makes up for purity of style with youthful ardor. And if they are not always up to the author's demands, their bout with him does them credit. Nonetheless . . . they sometimes attain the harmony that Synge intended. For these moments, alone, the production is well worth seeing. . . . Synge's retelling of the tale followed his expressed formula for writing 'stoicism, asceticism, and ecstasy'. When working on the play, he knew himself to be dying . . . leaving *Deirdre* still not quite polished to his satisfaction. . . .

The play reflects Synge's own consciousness of living close to death — symbolized most vividly by the newly-dug grave onstage in the third act — and his stoical acceptance of life's brief ecstasy. His asceticism is reflected in his restrained treatment, all the more moving, of the physical passion between Deirdre and Naisi, which is sung by the lovers rather than displayed. . . . Although the acting is not always inspired, the play itself is. Until a really brilliant production comes along, this one will do. On the whole, it's worth the trip down town.

Arthur Gelb, *New York Times*, 15 Oct. 1959

Scenarios, Dialogues, and Fragments

When the Moon Has Set

A young man on a walk in the country meets an old mad woman, Mary Costello, who frightens him with her wild talk. He returns to the large country house in which his uncle has just died and learns that the woman has gone mad because in earlier days she had, for religious reasons, rejected his uncle's love. He uses this instance and other arguments to persuade his uncle's nurse, a young and beautiful nun, sister Eileen, to give up the veil and marry him. Finally she discards her habit, and, putting on 'a green dress cut low at the neck', agrees to accept his love.

This play was begun with fragmentary notes in 1896-98, and a two-act version completed by the end of 1901. It was rejected by Yeats and Lady Gregory for a possible Abbey production. After this Synge appears to have reworked it, and he retained the typescripts and worksheets of the play when he tidied his papers before his death. He clearly intended them to be available for his literary executors to study. The play is reproduced in full in *Collected Works, Vol. III: Plays, Book 1*.

Plan for a Play

A scenario for a five-act play written in German (a language Synge was studying at the time), April-May 1894. Reproduced in a translation by E. M. Stephens, revised by Paul F. Botheroyd, in *Collected Works, Vol. III: Plays, Book 1*, p. 181-2.

A Rabelaisian Rhapsody

According to his diary entry of 14 Nov., Synge read *The Imitation of Christ* by Thomas à Kempis in 1896, and in 'J. M. Synge and the Ireland of His Time', Yeats records that Synge had intended to write a complete dramatic version. Only fragments of dialogue exist (see *Collected Works, Vol. III*, p. 183-6), and a statement suggesting the title: 'Here is my Rabelaisian rhapsody. I believe in gaiety which is surely a divine impulse peculiar to humanity and I think Rabelais is equal to any of the saints.'

Magna Serenitas (The Way of Peace)

A scenario for a three-act play which appears to have originated in an incident recorded in *The Aran Islands*, Part IV (see *Collected Works*,

Vol. II, p. 156). The dramatis personae and scenario are reproduced in *Collected Works, Vol. II*, p. 187-8.

A Vernal Play

In Fragment 1, set in a Wicklow glen, it is a 'soft kind morning on the hills' and two girls, Etain and Niave, are out picking wild flowers when they meet Cermuid and his wife Boinn. Afer some conversation filled with the mood of pastoral peace they are met by an Old Man who calls himself 'friend of love'. In Fragment 2, the Old Man having died, Etain, Boinn, and Niave 'rhyme and death rhyme' over him, reasserting love and joy in the natural world.

Three references occur to this verse play in Synge's diaries for 1902-03. It is reproduced in full in *Collected Works, Vol. I*, p. 69-73, and in *Collected Works, Vol. III*, p. 189-93.

Luasnad, Capa and Laine

On a bleak mountain as yet uncovered by the rising flood, every hope of escape or delivery is destroyed as soon as voiced. Luasnad gives birth to a child but it dies. Soon only Luasnad and Laine's wife are left alive. He tells her he loves her and they make love before they are swept away to their deaths.

Synge reviewed Geoffrey Keating's *The History of Ireland*, translated by David Comyn, for *The Speaker* in September 1902, and probably based this fragment on the tale of three fishermen in Book 1. The text is reproduced in *Collected Works, Vol. III*, p. 194-205.

Aughavanna Play

First referred to by Synge as 'Wicklow Play', 27 Jan. 1903, and amended to 'Aughavanna Play' on 3 Feb. Aughavanna is a valley in County Wicklow, and, according to Ann Saddlemyer, might serve as a setting for *The Tinker's Wedding* or *When the Moon Has Set*. A fragment of dialogue is included in *Collected Works, Vol. III*, p. 206-7.

The Lady O'Conor

Synge was first told the story of O'Conor and his lady by Pat Dirane, the old shanachie of Inishmaan. He wrote a prose version, 'A Story from Inishmaan', which was published in the *New Ireland Review* in November 1898, and this he later revised for inclusion in *The Aran Islands*,

Part I (see *Collected Works, Vol. II*, p. 61-3). Part of the text is included together with the scenario in *Collected Works, Vol. II*, p. 208-14.

Bride and Kathleen: a Play of '98

After the Irish Players' successful visit to London in March 1904, Frank Fay wrote to Synge encouraging him to write a play about the 1898 rebellion: 'Will you try the '98 play I was talking to you about? We must try to get an intelligent popular audience in Dublin. The people who might support us at sixpence a head are a good [deal] afraid that we are irreligious and politically unsound. We must do something to get them to believe in us. The same people come to show after show. . . . If you could, give us a drama of '98 as much alive as *In the Shadow of the Glen* and *Riders to the Sea* showing what the peasantry had to endure. I believe there were whole districts in which there was not a woman unviolated. I think Yeats in *Cathleen* has pointed out the right road for plays of that time. The leaders only give you melodrama; it is a picture of the smaller tyrannies that their followers had to endure that we want.' Synge replied: 'By all means have '98 plays — I will do one if I can — but *strong* and good dramas only will bring us people who are interested in the drama, and they are, after all, the people we must have.' In his essay 'J. M. Synge and the Ireland of His Time', Yeats records the company's reaction to Synge's scenario. It is reproduced with a fragment of dialogue in *Collected Works, Vol. III*, p. 215-17.

Deaf Mutes for Ireland

Two scenarios written while Synge was working on *Playboy*, possibly during the attacks on his plays by the *United Irishman* in 1904-05. The first scenario shows the import of the intended piece. The text is reproduced in *Complete Works, Vol. III, Book I*.

National Drama: a Farce

Set in a national club room with emblematic features (portraits of patriots, a map of Ireland and Hungary, a harp without strings, the head of a pike, and volumes of books bound in green), the action comprises a discussion in which various speakers assert that Irish drama should show 'the virtue of its country' and should 'have no sex,' and that playwrights should 'draw out their materials from the pearly depths of the Celtic imagination . . . leaving the naked truth a little to one side'. Jameson, who embodies Synge's views, responds in two long speeches.

This was probably written after *The Shadow of the Glen* had been attacked. Synge's executors ignored Yeats's memorandum to them: 'I remember the circumstance that made him write this, and could give it to his editor, or write a note myself if it seems important enough', and it was published for the first time in *Collected Works Vol. III* p. 220-6. Parts of Jameson's speeches are reproduced in 'The Writer on His Work', below.

Idea for a Play: 'A Struggle for Ireland'

This resulted from a visit in the summer of 1905 to the Blasket Islands, which Synge considered to be 'probably even more primitive than Aran'. On the Great Blasket he stayed with Shawn Keane, 'The King', whose life is described in Synge's essays published in *The Shanachie*, 1907 (see *Collected Works, Vol. II*, p. 247-57). The scenario, which has many resemblances to *Playboy*, is reproduced in *Complete Works, Vol. III, Book 1*.

Scenario : 'The Robbers'

Written at the same time as Synge's review of A. H. Leah's *Heroic Romances of Ireland*, published in the *Manchester Guardian*, 6 March 1906. The text is reproduced in *Complete Works, Vol. III, Book 1*.

Scenario: 'Thieves'

Although noted by Synge after the draft of 'The Vagrants of Wicklow', which was published in *The Shanachie* in Autumn 1906, the ideas were not further developed. See *Complete Works, Vol. III, Book 1*.

Comedy for Kings

Drawings and scenario probably noted during the autumn of 1906, and reproduced in *Complete Works, Vol. III*, p. 230.

Lucifer and the Lost Soul: a Mystery

Small fragment of dialogue reproduced in *Complete Works, Vol. III*, p. 231.

Poems

Published: with *Translations*, Dublin: Cuala Press, 1909, in a
limited edition of 250 copies, and New York: John Quinn,
in an edition of 50 copies; in *The Works of J. M. Synge,
Volume II* (Dublin: Maunsel, 1909); *Collected Works,
Vol. I: Poems*, ed. Robin Skelton (Oxford University Press,
1962), containing much previously unpublished material;
Plays, Poems, and Prose (London: Dent, 1992).

[Yeats was instrumental in the publication of the first edition,
a detailed account of which is given in Robin Skelton's
introduction to the *Collected Works, Vol. I*, and wrote a
preface to the first edition in which he observes that Synge
'once said to me, "We must unite asceticism, stoicism,
ecstacy; two of these often come together but not all three",
and the strength that made him delight in setting the hard
virtues by the soft, the bitter by the sweet, salt by mercury, the
stone by the elixir, gave him a hunger for harsh facts, for ugly
surprising things, for all that defies our hope.' Yeats
concluded: 'He was a solitary, undemonstrative man, never
asking pity, nor complaining, nor seeking sympathy but in this
book's momentary cries: all folded up in brooding intellect,
knowing nothing of new books and newspapers, reading the
great masters alone: and he was but the more hated because he
gave his country what it needed, an unmoved mind where
there is a perpetual last day, a trumpeting, and coming up to
judgement' (p. xxxiv-v). Yeats's preface was followed by one
from Synge. He had indicated his intentions to Yeats in a letter
accompanying the original manuscript: 'If I print them I would
possibly put a short preface to say that as there has been a
false "poetic diction" there has been and is a false "poetic
material". That if verse, even great verse, is to be alive it must
be occupied with the whole life — as it was with Villon and
Shakespeare's songs, and with Herrick and Burns. For
although exalted verse is the highest, it cannot keep its power
unless there is more essentially vital verse at the side of it, as
ecclesiastical architecture cannot remain fine when domestic
architecture is debased. Victor Hugo and Browning tried in a
way to get life into verse but they were without humour which
is the essentially poetic quality in what I call vital verse.'
(*Collected Works, Vol. I*, p. xv-xvi). A further extract from the
Preface is included in 'The Writer on His Work', below.]

The Aran Islands

Published: London: Elkin Matthews; Dublin: Maunsel, 1907, with
twelve drawings by Jack B. Yeats, simultaneously with a large-paper
limited edition of 150 copies, with Yeats's drawings coloured by
hand, signed by the author and artist; in *The Works of J. M. Synge,
Volume III* (Dublin: Maunsel, 1910), without Yeats's illustrations;
library edition (Dublin: Maunsel, 1911), with the drawings; in
Collected Works, Volume II: Prose, ed. Alan Price (Oxford
University Press, 1966); London: Allen and Unwin, 1968; ed.
Robin Skelton, illustrated with photographs by the author (Oxford
University Press, 1979); London: Penguin, 1992.

[Synge had been encouraged to visit the Aran Islands by Yeats when
they met in Paris in 1896: 'Give up Paris. You will never create anything
by reading Racine, and Arthur Symons will always be a better critic of
French literature. Go to the Aran Islands. Live there as if you were one
of the people themselves; express a life that has never found expression'
(*Collected Works, Vol. II*). Synge first visited Aran from 10 May to 25
June 1898, spending two weeks on Inishmore (Aranmor), and four on
Inishmaan. He returned in the summers of 1899, 1900, 1901, and 1902,
spending in all four and a half months on the islands. In letters to
Spencer Brodney on 10 and 12 December 1907, Synge wrote: 'I look on
The Aran Islands as my first serious piece of work — it was written
before any of my plays. In writing out the talk of the people and their
stories in this book, and in a certain number of articles on the Wicklow
peasantry which I have not yet collected, I learned to write the peasant
dialogue which I use in my plays. . . . *The Aran Islands* throws a good
deal of light on my plays' (*Collected Works, Vol. II*, p. 47).

In his Introduction Synge asserted: 'In the pages that follow I have
given a direct account of my life on the islands, and of what I met with
among them, inventing nothing, and changing nothing that is essential.
As far as possible, however, I have disguised the identity of the people I
speak of, by making changes in their names, and in the letters I quote,
and by altering some local and family relationships. I have had nothing
to say about them that was not wholly in their favour, but I have made
this disguise to keep them from ever feeling that a too direct use had
been made of their kindness, and friendship, for which I am more grateful than it is easy to say' (*Collected Works, Vol. II*, p. 47-8).

The book is neither objective nor intended as a 'tourist guide' to the
islands. It is written in journal form, divided into four sections, each
focusing on one visit to the area, and narrated in the first person. The
narrator shares the islanders' 'primitive' sensibility, appreciative of both
the beautiful and the grotesque. He vividly describes the islands'

isolation, the desolation of the landscape, and the awesome power of the sea; the simplicity and solitude of the islanders' lives, their belief in the supernatural, and their constant awareness of death. This is contrasted with their humour, the vitality of the islanders' culture, and their conviction of its strength and survival. In a passage in Notebook 19 (perhaps considered too 'political' for inclusion in the final text), Synge reveals the depth of his involvement in and concern for the destiny of the Aran Islands and their people: 'The thought that this island will gradually yield to the ruthlessness of "progress" is as the certainty that decaying age is moving always nearer the cheeks it is your ecstasy to kiss. How much of Ireland was formerly like this and how much of Ireland is today Anglicized and civilized and brutalized? . . . Am I not leaving in Inishmaan spiritual treasure unexplored whose presence is as a great magnet to my soul? In this ocean alone is not every symbol of the cosmos?' (*Collected Works, Vol. II*, p. 103). For an account of the book's publication, see Lady Gregory's *Our Irish Theatre* (Gerrards Cross: Colin Smythe, 1972), p. 76-8.]

In Wicklow, West Kerry and Connemara

Published: in *The Works of John M. Synge* (Dublin: Maunsel, 1910); separate library edition, Dublin: Maunsel, 1911, excluding 'Under Ether', and including eight drawings by Jack B. Yeats; in *Collected Works, Volume II: Prose*, ed. Alan Price (Oxford University Press, 1966), based on the text of the 1911 library edition, with additions to five essays and two extra essays; Dublin: O'Brien Press, 1980, with essays by Ann Saddlemyer and George Gmelch, and photographs by George Gmelch.

[*In Wicklow, West Kerry and Connemara* consists of articles by Synge collected posthumously, the selection of which was the cause of a quarrel between W. B. Yeats and George Roberts, a director of Maunsel and Company. An account of this dispute is given by Alan Price in his introduction to *Collected Works, Vol. II: Prose*, p. xiii-xiv.

In her introductory essay to the O'Brien Press edition, Ann Saddlemyer cites passages from Part One, *In Wicklow*, in which 'we find the source for Nora's intensity in *The Shadow of the Glen*, her oppression as the fog lifts momentarily only to overwhelm her again in "the sense of loneliness has no equal" (p. 57), her instant communion with the strange Tramp who has come to terms with this constantly evolving environment'.]

For such travellers, 'the strained feeling of regret one has so often in these places' (p. 39) is delicately balanced by the equally solitary splendour afforded by a glimpse of 'a handful of jagged sky filled with extraordinarily brilliant stars' (p. 45). And once again the bewildering fluctuation of atmosphere is in turn a constant reminder of the broader spectrums still, of seasons and time itself. 'In these hills the summer passes in a few weeks from a late spring, full of odour and colour, to an autumn that is premature and filled with the desolate splendour of decay', Synge writes in 'The Vagrants of Wicklow'. It is this knowledge of transience that makes old Mary Byrne of *The Tinker's Wedding* wise and Sarah Casey restless. . . . Synge's essays in Part Two, *In West Kerry*, reflect the same compassion for a life daring and basic in its simplicity, sharpened even further by the harsh breathtaking grandeur of the desolate surroundings. . . . But perhaps nowhere more successfully than in *The Playboy of the Western World* do we find the full range of mood from that 'strange feeling of loneliness' to the romance the young Blasket girls found in a face 'still raw and bleeding and horrible to look at'. The combinations of lyricism and earthiness, sudden surprise, and sharp sensibilities developed in the prose essays are skilfully echoed in a rising series of actions and swooping dialogue steadily widening in range while increasing in intensity and outrageous candour. . . . Synge placed his bitter-sweet comedy in the wilds of Mayo, but the sentiments reflect his travels throughout Ireland and particularly west Kerry, which he visited during the writing of *The Playboy*. The 'singularly brilliant liveliness one meets everywhere in Kerry' (p. 91) is woven also through his rollicking sunlit Wicklow farce, *The Tinker's Wedding*, whose principles confront law and clergy in much the same mood as the old flower-woman challenges the police in the barrack yard and the drunken Blasket Islanders carelessly face the elements on their way home from the fair, or the brawling after the sandhill races.

Ann Saddlemyer, Introduction,
In Wicklow, West Kerry and Connemara (1980), p. 21-3

Other Prose Pieces

Autobiographical

The following prose pieces were collected together for the first time by Alan Price in *Collected Works, Vol. II: Prose*, Part One, 'The Man Himself' (Oxford University Press, 1966).

'Autobiography'. Alan Price's version of the *Autobiography* was first published by the Dolmen Press, Dublin, in 1965, constructed from notebooks and manuscripts left by Synge. In his introduction Alan Price writes: 'Synge made several attempts at writing autobiography. It is not certain why he did not bring them together in a finished whole and seek publication. Maybe they did not reach the high standard he required; maybe they were too self-revealing — he did not wish "Vita Vecchia" or "Etude Morbide" [see below] to appear during his life-time, even though the autobiographical elements in them were veiled. Still, fortunately, the drafts of autobiography remain among his unpublished writing' (p. xi). The work covers his childhood, adolescence, and early student days, and reveals his struggle with religious belief, his love of nature, and his passion for music. Several passages are quoted in the section 'The Writer on His Work', below.

'Vita Vecchia'. Written between 1895 and 1897, and partly revised later, probably in 1907, this comprises fourteen poems connected by prose narrative.

'Etude Morbide'. Written about 1899, and revised probably in 1907. In a footnote to *Collected Works, Vol. II*, Alan Price observes that the two foregoing pieces 'continue Synge's account of his life, though in a veiled and subjective form'. He quotes Synge —'The story is not one that I would care to narrate in all particulars' — and continues: 'They present his interior difficulties and growth, his spiritual and artistic condition and strivings, and his feelings about the women who were important to him during the years when he lived a good deal on the Continent'. Price interprets the pieces as 'the expression of dreams and ideas, longings and discoveries, rather than a record of actual lives or material events'. He again quotes Synge: 'This is a story I have inscribed in verses called "Vita Vecchia" which is a series of dreams of my later life as told in the study I am now trying to finish.' The 'study' referred to here is 'Etude Morbide', mentioned by Synge in a letter to Yeats which he wrote before undergoing his operation in 1908: 'I am a little bothered about my papers. . . . I wonder could you get someone . . . to go through them for you and do whatever you and Lady Gregory think desirable. It is rather a hard thing to ask you, but I do not want my good things destroyed, or my bad things printed rashly — especially a morbid thing about a mad fiddler in Paris, which I hate.'

'On a Train to Paris'. Price's own conflation of two separate versions, probably written about 1897. The title is not Synge's own.

'Under Ether', sub-titled 'Personal Experiences during an Operation'. First published in *The Works of J. M. Synge, Vol. III* (Dublin: Maunsel, 1910). In December 1897 Synge underwent an operation for the removal of swollen glands in his neck (for details, see 'Brief Chronology', p. 9, above). Synge wrote this essay soon afterwards.

Literary and Other Essays

Most of the following essays, which originally appeared in periodicals in Ireland, France, and England between 1898 and 1906, were collected together for the first time by Alan Price in *Collected Works, Vol. II: Prose*, Part Four, 'About Literature' (Oxford University Press, 1966). Also included are some previously unpublished prose pieces.

'Various Notes'. Ten observations by Synge on the nature of literature. He begins: 'All theorizing is bad for the artist, because it makes him live in the intelligence instead of in the half subconscious faculties by which all real creation is performed' (p. 347).

'La Vielle Litterature Irlandaise', *L'Européan*, 15 March 1902.

'The Poems of Geoffrey Keating', *The Speaker*, 8 December 1900. A review of *Danta Amhrain in Caointe, Sheathruin Ceitinn* (*Poems, Songs, and Keens of Geoffrey Keating*), an important volume according to Synge, since it was 'the first collected edition of the works of a Gaelic poet that has ever been given to the public'.

'An Irish Historian', *The Speaker*, 6 September 1902. A review of *Foras Feasa Ar Eirinn* (*The History of Ireland*), by Geoffrey Keating.

'Celtic Mythology', *The Speaker*, 2 April 1904. A review of *The Irish Mythological Cycle and Celtic Mythology*, by H. D'Arbois de Jubainville, a leading Celtic scholar whose lectures Synge attended at the Sorbonne in 1898 and 1902.

'An Epic of Ulster', *The Speaker*, 7 June 1902. A review of Lady Gregory's *Culchulain of Muirthemne*. Synge declares himself hopeful that 'This version of the epic tales relating to Culchulain, the Irish mythical hero, should go far to make a new period in the intellectual life of Ireland. Henceforward the beauty and wonder of the old literature is likely to have an influence on the culture of all classes.'

'A Translation of Irish Romance', *Manchester Guardian*, 28 December 1905. A review of A. H. Leahy's *Heroic Romances of Ireland, Vol. I*.

'Irish Heroic Romance', *Manchester Guardian*, 6 March 1906. A review of A. H. Leahy's *Heroic Romances of Ireland, Vol. II*.

'Irish Fairy Stories', *The Speaker*, 21 June 1902. A review of Seumas MacManus's *Donegal Fairy Stores*.

'Le Mouvement Intellectuel Irlandais', *L'Europeam*, 31 May 1902.

'The Old and New in Ireland', *The Academy and Literature*, VI (September 1902). A perceptive appraisal of the Irish literary renaissance and Gaelic revival.

'The Fair Hills of Ireland', *Manchester Guardian*, 16 November 1906. A review of Stephen Gwynn's *The Fair Hills of Ireland*.

'The Winged Destiny', *The Academy and Literature*, 12 November 1904. A review of Fiona Macleod's *The Winged Destiny*.

'A Celtic Theatre', *The Freeman's Journal*, 22 March 1900. Most of this article focuses on Anatole Le Braz's account of a production of a play in Brittany. However, in the opening paragraphs Synge remarks: 'It is strange that the Celtic races should have evolved about the same time a unique body of actors in Brittany, and a few poets in Ireland who are producing works that seem incomplete when played with the accent and tradition of the London stage. Unfortunately, the players act in Breton, and our poets write in English' (p. 393).

'Anatole Le Braz', *The Daily Express* (Dublin), 28 January 1899.

'The French Writers', conflated from 'Loti and Huysmans', *The Speaker*, 18 April 1901, and 'A Tale of Comedians', an unpublished article on Anatole France. The title is not Synge's.

'A Note on Boucicault and Irish Drama', *Academy and Literature,* 11 June 1904. Published in the 'Literary Notes' section: an 'interesting comparison between the methods of the early Irish melodrama and those of the Irish National Theatre Society'.

'Can We Go Back into our Mother's Womb', sub-titled 'A Letter to the Gaelic League, by a Hedge Schoolmaster'. Written in 1907 after *The Playboy*. Previously unpublished: an extract is included in the section 'The Writer on His Work', below.

'A Letter About J. M. Synge by Jack B. Yeats', *Evening Sun* (New York), 20 July 1909. A version of this under the title 'With Synge in Connemara' appears in W. B. Yeats's *J. M. Synge and the Ireland of His Time* (Dundrum: Cuala Press, 1911). Quoted earlier in this section.

Translations

Published: with *Poems*, Dublin: Cuala Press, 1909, in a limited edition of 250 copies, and New York: John Quinn, in an edition of 50 copies; in *The Works of J. M. Synge, Volume II* (Dublin: Maunsel, 1910); *J. M. Synge: Translations*, ed. Robin Skelton (Dublin: Dolmen Press, 1961), in an edition of 750 copies, including previously unpublished material; *Collected Works, Vol. I*, ed. Robin Skelton (Oxford University Press, 1962).

[In his Preface to the first, Cuala edition, Synge writes: 'The translations are sometimes free, and sometimes almost literal, according as seemed most fitting with the form of language I have used.']

I was painfully timid, and while still very young, the idea of Hell took a fearful hold on me. One night I thought I was irretrievably damned and cried myself to sleep in vain yet terrified efforts to form a conception of eternal pain. In the morning I renewed my lamentations and my mother was sent for. She comforted me with the assurance that the Holy Ghost was convicting me of sin and thus preparing me for ultimate salvation. This was a new idea, and I rather approved.

'Autobiography', *Collected Works, Vol. II: Prose*, p. 14

When I was about fourteen I obtained a book of Darwin's. It opened in my hands at a passage where he asks how can we explain the similarity between a man's hand and a bird's or bat's wings except by evolution. I flung the book aside and rushed out into the open air — it was summer and we were in the country — the sky seeemed to have lost its blue and the grass its green. I lay down and writhed in an agony of doubt. My studies showed me the force of what I read, [and] the more I put it from me the more it rushed back with new instances and power. Till then I had never doubted and never conceived that a sane and wise man or boy could doubt. I had of course heard of atheists but as vague monsters that I was unable to realize. It seemed that I was become in a moment the playfellow of Judas. Incest and parricide were but a consequence of the idea that possessed me. My memory does not record how I returned home nor how long my misery lasted. I know only that I got the book out of the house as soon as possible and kept it out of sight, saying to myself logically enough that I was not yet sufficiently advanced in science to weigh his arguments, so I would do better to reserve his work for future study. In a few weeks or so I regained my composure, but this was the beginning. Soon afterwards I turned my attention to works of Christian evidence, reading them at first with pleasure, soon with doubt, and at last in some cases with derision. . . . This story is easily told, but it was a terrible experience. By it I laid a chasm between my present and my past and between myself and my kindred and friends. Till I was twenty-three I never met or at least knew a man or woman who shared my opinions.

'Autobiography', *Collected Works, Vol. II: Prose*, p. 10-11

In my childhood the presence of furze bushes and rocks and flooded streams and strange mountain fogs and sunshine gave me a strange sense of enchantment and delight but I think when I [rested] on a mountain I sat quite as gladly looking on the face of a boulder as at the finest view of glen and river. . . . I think the consciousness of beauty is awakened in persons as in peoples by a prolonged unsatisfied desire. . . . Perhaps the modern feeling for the beauty of nature as a particular quality — an expression of divine ecstasy rather than a mere decoration of the world — arose when men began to look on everything about them with the unsatisfied longing which has its proper analogue in puberty. . . . The feeling everyone will recognize in Wordsworth's *Ode*, though he does not seem perhaps to give it its truest interpretation.,

'Autobiography', *Collected Works, Vol. II: Prose*, p. 12-13

We do wrong to seek a foundation for ecstasy in philosophy or the hidden things of the spirit — if there is spirit — for when life is at its simplest, with nothing beyond or before it, the mystery is greater than we can endure.

'Vita Vecchia', *Collected Works, Vol. II: Prose*, p. 24

One evening when I was collecting on the brow of a long valley in County Wicklow wreaths of white mist began to rise from the narrow bogs beside the river. Before it was quite dark I looked round the edge of the field and saw two immense luminous eyes looking at me from the base of the valley. I dropped my net and caught hold of a gate in front of me. Behind the eyes there rose a black sinister forehead. I was fascinated. For a moment the eyes seemed to consume my personality, then the whole valley became filled with a pageant of movement and colour, and the opposite hillside covered itself with ancient doorways and spires and high turrets. I did not know where or when I was existing. At last someone spoke in the lane behind me — it was a man going home — and came back to myself. The night had become quite dark and the eyes were no longer visible, yet I recognized in a moment what had caused the apparition — two clearings in a wood lined with white mist divided again by a few trees which formed the eye-balls. For many days afterwards I could not look on these fields even in daylight without terror.

'Autobiography', *Collected Works, Vol. I : Prose*, p. 10

All living things demand their share of joy, and I see no permanent joy apart from the creation or touching of beautiful forms or ideas. This is the immortal fragment of religion. As art may decorate what is useful or exist for its own beauty in itself, so an action done with a beautiful motive is decorated and joyful, and for souls that are barred from the joy of activity there is still the quiescent ecstasy of resignation. . . . I am hearing many ghost stories. Since I have come back to nature my rather crude materialism has begun to dissatisfy me. Nature is miraculous and my own dreams were something extra-human. . . . I am yielding up my imagination to the marvellous. These things cannot be understood without an intimate if cautious sympathy, and I long to lift the veil and to see with my own inward sight the pretended symbols of the soul. . . . I have come out among the hills to write music again if I am able. . . . All art that is not conceived by a soul in harmony with some mood of the earth is without value, and unless we are able to produce a myth more beautiful than nature — holding in itself a spiritual grace beyond and through the earthly — it is better to be silent.

'Etude Morbide', *Collected Works, Vol. II: Prose*, p. 31-5

In short you think that the Irish drama should hold up the mirror to the Irish nation and it going to Mass on a fine springdayish Sunday morning? . . . I have not much to say. An Irish drama that is written in Ireland about Irish people, and not on a foreign model, will and must be national in so far as it exists at all. Our hope of it is that as Ireland is a beautiful and lovely country that the drama that Ireland is now producing may catch a little of this beauty and loveliness, as the Irish music has caught it [without] knowing or thinking, and will escape the foolishness that all wilful national[ism] is so full of. . . . Art is sad or gay, religious or heretical, by reason of accident and cause we cannot account for and the small Tuscany produced at one time Dante and Boccaccio, who are surely both national and yet we feel that Dante might have been born in Paris or Rabelais in Venice. The national element in art is merely the colour, the intensity of the wildness or restraint of the humour. . . . I do not say that all artistic production is national — Gaelic adaptations (imitations) of fourth-rate English poetry are not national because they are not anything. . . . If you do not like a work that is passing itself off as national art you had better show that it is not art. If it is good art it is in vain for you to try and show that is not national. . . . If we get drunk a little more in public than the other nations of Europe, would you have us reeling on the stage in order that we may be national? No? Then if we have a few little fragments of local virtue must [they] be paraded in our button holes like a Gaelic button? The essentials of all art are the eternal human elements (coat sleeve) of humanity which are the same everywhere, and it is only in the attributes that make an art more or less charged with beauty, more or less daring and exquisite in form, more or [less] dull or shiny on its surface, that the influence of place is to be found. . . .

'National Drama: a Farce', *Collected Works, Vol. III*, p. 224-6

Dramatic art is first of all a childish art — a reproduction of external experience — without form or philosophy; then after a lyrical interval we have it as mature drama dealing with the deeper truth of general life in a perfect form and with mature philosophy.

There are sides of all that western life the groggy-patriot-publican-general shop-man who is married to the priest's half-sister and is second cousin once-removed of the dispensary doctor, that are horrible and awful. This is the type that is running the present United Irish League anti-grazier campaign, while they're swindling the people themselves in a dozen ways and then buying out their holdings and packing off whole families to America. The subject is too big to go into here, but at best it's beastly. All that side of the matter of course I left untouched, in my stuff. I sometimes wish to God I hadn't a soul and then I could give myself up to putting those lads on the stage. God, wouldn't they hop! In a way it is all heartrending, in one place the people are starving but wonderfully attractive and charming, and in another place where things are going well, one has a rampant, double-chinned vulgarity I haven't seen the life of.

> From a letter to Stephen MacKenna, *Irish Rennaissance*
> (Dublin: Dolmen Press, 1965), p. 72-3.

Man is naturally a nomad . . . and all wanderers have finer intellectual and physical perceptions than men who are condemned to local habitations. The cycle, automobile, and conducted tours are half-conscious efforts to replace the charm of the stage coach and of pilgrimages like Chaucer's. But the vagrant, I think, along with perhaps the sailor has preserved the dignity of motion with its whole sensation of strange colours in the clouds and of strange passages with voices that whisper in the dark and still stranger inns and lodgings, affections and lonely songs that rest for a whole life time with the perfume of spring evenings or the first autumnal smoulder of the leaves. . . . There is something grandiose in a man who has forced all kingdoms of the earth to yield the tribute of his bread and who, at a hundred, begs on the wayside with the pride of an emperor. The slave and beggar are wiser than the man who works for recompense, for all our moments are divine and above all price though their sacrifice is paid with a measure of fine gold. Every industrious worker has sold his birthright for a mess of pottage, perhaps served him in chalices of gold. . . .

> *In Wicklow, West Kerry and Connemara*,
> *Collected Works, Vol. II*, p. 195-6

The tragedy of the landlord class . . . and of the innumerable old families that are quickly dwindling away. These owners of the land are not much pitied at the present day or much deserving of pity; and yet one cannot quite forget that they are the descendants of what was at one time in the eighteenth century a high-spirited and highly-cultivated aristocracy. The broken greenhouses and mouse-eaten libraries, that were designed and collected by men who voted with Grattan, are perhaps as mournful in the end as the four mud walls that are so often left in Wicklow as the only remnants of a farmhouse. . . . Many of the descendants of these people have, of course, drifted into professional life in Dublin, or have gone abroad; yet, wherever they are, they do not equal their forefathers, and where men used to collect fine editions of *Don Quixote* and Molière, in Spanish and French, and luxuriantly bound copies of Juvenal and Persius and Cicero, nothing is read now but Longfellow and Hall Caine and Miss Corelli. Where good and roomy houses were built a hundred years ago, poor and tawdry houses are built now; and bad bookbindings, bad pictures, and bad decorations are thought well of, where rich bindings, beautiful miniatures, and finely-carved chimney pieces were once prized by the old Irish landlords.

'A Landlord's Garden in County Wicklow',
In Wicklow, West Kerry and Connemara, as above, p. 231

The religious art is a thing of the past only — a vain and foolish regret — and its place has been taken by our quite modern feeling for the beauty and mystery [of] nature, an emotion that has gradually risen up as religion in the dogmatic sense has gradually died. Our pilgrimages are not to Canterbury or Jerusalem, but to Killarney and Cumberland and the Alps. . . .

Man has gradually grown up in this world that is about us, and I think that while Tolstoy is wrong in claiming that art should be intelligible to the peasant, he is right in seeking a criterion for the arts, and I think this is to be found in testing art by its compatibility with the outside world and the peasants or people who live near it. A book, I mean, that one feels ashamed to read in a cottage of Dingle Bay one may fairly call a book that is not healthy — or universal.

'Various Notes', *Collected Works, Vol. II: Prose*, p. 351

Poetry roughly is of two kinds, the poetry of real life — the poetry of Burns, and Shakespeare, Villon, and the poetry of a land of the fancy — the poetry of Spenser and Keats and Ronsard. That is obvious enough, but what is highest in poetry is always reached where the dreamer is leaning out to reality or where the man of real life is lifted out of it. . . .

In these days poetry is usually a flower of evil or good, but it is the timber of poetry that wears most surely, and there is no timber that has not strong roots amongst the clay and worms. Even if we grant that exalted poetry can be kept successful by itself, the strong things of life are needed in poetry also, to show that what is exalted, or tender, is not made by feeble blood. It may almost be said that before verse can be human again it must learn to be brutal.

Collected Works, Vol. I: Poems, p. xiv-xv, xxxvi

a: Primary Sources

Collected Editions

Collected Works (Oxford University Press, 1962-68; reprinted, Gerrards Cross: Colin Smythe, 1982), comprising:

> *Volume I: Poems*, ed. Robin Skelton, 1962. [Part One: Poems; Part Two: Poetic Drama, including *The Vernal Play*, *The Lady O'Conor*, and *Luasnad, Capa and Laine*; Part Three: Translations.]
>
> *Volume II: Prose*, ed. Alan Price, 1966. [Part One: 'The Man Himself' (autobiographical pieces); Part Two: *The Aran Islands*; Part Three: *In Wicklow, West Kerry and Connemara*; Part Four: 'About Literature' (essays).]
>
> *Volume III: Plays, Book 1*, ed. Ann Saddlemyer, 1968. [*Riders to the Sea*, *The Shadow of the Glen*, *The Well of the Saints*, and *When the Moon Has Set*.]
>
> *Volume IV: Plays, Book 2*, ed. Ann Saddlemyer, 1968. [*The Tinker's Wedding*, *The Playboy of the Western World*, and *Deirdre of the Sorrows*.]

Plays, Poems, and Prose, with an introduction by Michéal MacLiammoir (London: Dent, 1958); revised edition, ed. and with an introduction by Alison Smith, and preface by Michéal MacLiammoir, London: Dent, 1992. [The fullest conveniently accessible edition.]

Four Plays and the Aran Islands, ed. Robin Skelton (London: Oxford University Press, 1962).

The Plays and Poems of J. M. Synge, ed. T. R. Henn (London: Methuen, 1963).

The Complete Plays, with an introduction and notes by T. R. Henn (London: Methuen, 1981).

Editions of Individual Works

Riders to the Sea, ed. Robin Skelton (London: Oxford University Press, 1969).

Riders to the Sea and Playboy of the Western World, ed. Alan Price (Oxford: Basil Blackwell, 1969).

The Playboy of the Western World (Dublin: Mercier Press, 1974). [Includes an introduction by the actor Eamonn Keane on playing Christy.]

The Playboy of the Western World, New Mermaids series,
    ed. Malcolm Kelsall (London: Ernest Benn, 1975).
The Playboy of the Western World, Methuen Student Edition, with
    commentary and notes by Non Worrall (London: Methuen, 1983).
The Playboy of the Western World and Two Other Irish Plays (London:
    Penguin, 1987), first published as *Classic Irish Drama*, 1964. [Also
    includes Yeats's *The Countess Cathleen* and O'Casey's *Cock-a-
    Doodle Dandy*.]
The Playboy of the Western World and Riders to the Sea (London:
    Routledge, 1990).

Travel Writings

The Aran Islands (London: Allen and Unwin, 1968).
The Aran Islands, ed. Robin Skelton (London: Oxford University Press,
    1979). [Illustrated with photographs by the author.]
The Aran Islands (Penguin Classics, 1992).
In Connemara (Dublin: Mercier Press, 1979).
In Wicklow, West Kerry and Connemara (Dublin: O'Brien Press, 1980).
    [Includes essays by George Gmelch and Ann Saddlemyer, and
    photographs by George Gmelch.]

Collections of Letters

Letters to Molly: *John Millington Synge to Maire O'Neill 1906-1907*,
    ed. Ann Saddlemyer (Cambridge, Mass.: Belknap Press of Harvard
    University, 1971).
Collected Letters, Volume 1: 1871-1907, ed. Ann Saddlemyer (Oxford:
    Clarendon Press, 1983).
Collected Letters, Volume 2: 1907-1909, ed. Ann Saddlemyer (Oxford:
    Clarendon Press, 1984).

b: Secondary Sources

Background Works

Fay, Gerard, *The Abbey Theatre* (Dublin: Clonmore and Reynolds,
    1958).
Fay, W. G., and Carswell, Catherine, *The Fays of the Abbey Theatre: an
    Autobiographical Record* (London: Rich and Cowan, 1935).

A Select Bibliography

Fallis, Richard, *The Irish Renaissance: an Introduction to Anglo-Irish Literature* (Dublin: Gill and Macmillan, 1978).

Flannery, James W., *Miss Annie Horniman and the Abbey Theatre* (Dublin: Dolmen Press, 1970).

Hogan, Robert, and O'Neill, Michael J., *Joseph Holloway's Abbey Theatre* (Carbondale: Southern Illinois University Press, 1967).

Hogan, Robert, and Kilroy, James, *The Irish Literary Theatre 1899-1901* (Dublin: Dolmen Press, 1975).

Hogan, Robert, and Kilroy, James, *Laying the Foundations 1902-1904* (Dublin: Dolmen Press, 1976).

Hunt, Hugh, *The Abbey: Ireland's National Theatre* (London: Gill and Macmillan, 1979).

Lyons, F. S. L., *Culture and Anarchy in Ireland, 1890-1939* (Oxford University Press, 1982).

MacLiammoir, Mícheál, *Theatre in Ireland* (Dublin: Three Candles, 1964).

McMinna, Joseph, ed., *The Internationalism of Irish Literature and Drama*, Irish Literary Studies, 41 (Gerrards Cross: Colin Smythe, 1992).

Malone, A. E., *Irish Drama* (New York: Benjamin Blom, 1965).

Mercier, Vivian, *The Irish Comic Tradition* (Oxford: Clarendon Press. 1962).

Moore, George, 'Yeats, Lady Gregory, and Synge, II', *The English Review*, XVI (Feb. 1914), p. 350-64.

O'Connor, Ulick, *All the Olympians: a Biographical Portrait of the Irish Literary Renaissance* (New York: Henry Holt, 1984).

O'Driscoll, Robert, ed., *Theatre and Nationalism in Twentieth-Century Ireland* (University of Toronto Press, 1971).

Robinson, Lennox, *Ireland's Abbey Theatre: a History 1899-1951* (London: Sidgwick and Jackson, 1951).

Skelton, Robin, and Clark, David R., *Irish Renaissance* (Dublin: Dolmen Press, 1965).

Full-Length Studies

Ayling, Ronald, ed., *J. M. Synge: Four Plays*, Casebook series (London: Macmillan, 1992).

Benson, Eugene, *J. M. Synge*, Macmillan Modern Dramatists series (London: Macmillan, 1982).

Coxhead, Elizabeth, *J. M. Synge and Lady Gregory* (London: Longman, 1962, 1969).

Gerstenberger, Donna, *John Millington Synge*, Twayne's English Authors series (Boston: Twayne, 1990).

Greene, D. H. and Stephens, E. M., *J.M. Synge 1871-1909* (New York University Press, 1989).

Grene, Nicholas, *Synge: a Critical Study of the Plays* (London: Macmillan, 1975).

Harmon, Maurice, ed., *J. M. Synge Centenary Papers 1971* (Dublin: Dolmen Press, 1971).

Hogan, Robert, and Kilroy, James, *The Abbey Theatre: the Years of Synge, 1905-1909* (Dublin: Dolmen Press, 1978).

Johnson, Toni O'Brien, *Synge: the Medieval and the Grotesque* (Gerrards Cross: Colin Smythe, 1982).

Kilroy, James, *The Playboy Riots* (Dublin: Dolmen Press, 1971).

Mikhail, E. H., ed., *J. M. Synge: Interviews and Recollections* (London: Macmillan, 1977).

Price, Alan, *Synge and Anglo-Irish Drama* (London: Methuen, 1961).

Saddlemyer, Ann, *Synge and Modern Comedy* (Dublin: Dolmen Press, 1968).

Skelton, Robin, *The Writings of J. M. Synge* (New York: Bobbs-Merrill, 1971).

Skelton, Robin, *J. M. Synge and His World* (London: Thames and Hudson, 1971).

Strong, L. A. G., *John Millington Synge* (London: Allen and Unwin, 1941).

Symons, Samuel, *Letters to My Daughter*: *Memories of John Millington Synge*.

Whitaker, T. R., ed., *Twentieth-Century Interpretations of The Playboy of the Western World* (Englewood Cliffs, N. J.: Prentice-Hall, 1969).

Chapters in Books

Deane, Seamus, 'Synge and Heroism', *Celtic Revivals* (London: Faber, 1985), p. 51- 62.

Ellis-Fermor, Una, 'John Millington Synge', *The Irish Dramatic Movement* (London: Methuen, 1939), p. 163-86.

Fitz-Simon, Christopher, 'Great Literature in a Barbarous Idiom, 1903-1913: John Millington Synge and His Followers', *The Irish Theatre* (Thames and Hudson, 1983), p. 150-7.

Gregory, Lady, 'Synge' and '*The Playboy* in America', *Our Irish Theatre* (Gerrards Cross: Colin Smythe, 1972), p. 73-83, 97-135.

Maxwell, D. E. S., 'W. B. Yeats and J. M. Synge', *A Critical History of Modern Irish Drama, 1891-1980* (Cambridge University Press, 1984), p. 33-59.

O'Casey, Sean, 'John Millington Synge', *Blasts and Benedictions* (London: Macmillan, 1967).

O'Connor, Frank, 'Synge', *The Irish Theatre: Lectures Delivered during the Abbey Theatre Festival* (Dublin, 1938); ed. Lennox Robinson (London: Macmillan, 1939), p. 29-52.

Oh Aodaha, Michael, 'Synge and the Abbey Plays', *Theatre in Ireland* (Oxford: Basil Blackwell, 1974), p. 40-59.

Roche, Anthony, 'The Two Worlds of Synge's *The Well of the Saints*', *The Genres of the Irish Literary Revival*, ed. Ronald Schleifer (Dublin: Wolfhound Press, 1980), p. 27-38.

Weygandt, Cornelius, 'John Millington Synge', *Irish Plays and Playwrights* (Westport: Greenwood Press, 1979), p. 160-97.

Worth, Katharine, 'Synge', *The Irish Drama of Europe from Yeats to Beckett* (London: Athlone Press, 1978), p. 120-39.

Yeats, John Butler, 'Synge and the Irish', *Essays Irish and American* (Dublin: Talbot Press; London: T. F. Unwin; New York: Macmillan, 1918), p. 51-61.

Yeats, W. B., *The Cutting of an Agate* (London: Macmillan, 1919). [Includes 'The Tragic Theatre', p. 25-35; 'Preface to the First Edition of *The Well of the Saints*', p. 111-22; 'Preface to the First Edition of John Millington Synge's Poems and Translations', p. 123-9; 'J. M. Synge and the Ireland of His Time', p. 130-76.]

Yeats, W. B., *The Death of Synge, and Other Passages from an Old Diary* (Dublin: Cuala Press, 1928; reprinted, London: Macmillan, 1936).

Yeats, W. B., *Essays* (London: Macmillan, 1924). [Includes 'The Tragic Theatre', p. 294-6; 'Preface to the First Edition of *The Well of the Saints*', p. 369-78; 'Preface to the First Edition of John Millington Synge's Poems and Translations', p. 379-84; 'J. M. Synge and the Ireland of His Time', p. 385-424. Also reprinted in *Essays and Introductions* (London: Macmillan, 1961).]

Papers and Essays in Journals

Freyer, Grattan, 'The Little World of J. M. Synge', *Politics and Letters,* I, No. 4 (1948), p. 50-2.

Ganz, A., 'J. M. Synge and the Drama of Art', *Modern Drama,* X (1967), p. 57-68.

Gerstenberger, Donna, 'Bonnie and Clyde and Christy Mahon: Playboys All', *Modern Drama,* XIV (1971), p. 227-31.

Gorki, Maxim, 'Observations on the Theatre', *English Review,* XXXVIII (1942), p. 494-8.

Greene, D. H., '*The Tinker's Wedding*: a Revaluation', *PMLA,* LXII (1947), p. 824-7.

Harmon, Maurice, ed., *The Celtic Master* (Dublin: Dolmen Press, 1969).

Kilroy, J. F., 'The Playboy as Poet', *PMLA*, LXXIII (1968), p. 439-42.

Levitt, Paul M., 'The Structural Craftsmanship of J. M. Synge's *Riders to the Sea*', *Eire – Ireland*, IV (1969), p. 53-61.

Maclean, Hugh H., 'The Letters as Playboy', *University of Kansas City Review*, XXI (1954), p. 9-19.

O'Cuisin, S., 'J. M. Synge: His Art and Message', *Sinn Fein*, 17 July 1909.

Pearce, H. D., 'Synge's Playboy as Mock-Christ', *Modern Drama*, VIII (1965), p. 303-10.

Rit, Malcolm, '*Riders to the Sea*', *English Studies*, XLIX (1968), p. 445-9.

Sanderlin, R. R., 'Synge's *Playboy* and the Ironic Hero', *Southern Quarterly*, VI (1968), p. 289-301.

Sanduleson, George C., 'Synge's *The Aran Islands*: a World of Grey', Princess Grace Irish Library Lectures, No. 8 (Gerrards Cross: Colin Smythe, 1991).

Sidnell, M. J., 'Synge's *Playboy* and the Champion of Ulster', *Dalhousie Review*, XLV (1965), p. 51-9.

Spacks, P. M., 'The Making of *The Playboy*', *Modern Drama*, IV (1961), p. 314-23.

Sullivan, M. R., 'Synge, Sophocles, and the Un-Making of Myth', *Modern Drama*, XII (1969), p. 242-53.

Bibliographies

Ayling, Ronald, 'Select Bibliography', in *J. M. Synge: Four Plays* (London: Macmillan, 1992).

Bourgeois, Maurice, 'General Bibliography', in *John Millington Synge and the Irish Theatre* (London: Constable, 1913; New York: Benjamin Blom, 1965; Haskell House, 1966), p. 251-314.

Breed, Paul F., and Sanderman, Florence M., eds., *John Millington Synge: Dramatic Criticism* (Detroit: Gale Research, 1972), p. 685-93.

Eager, Anan R., *A Guide to Irish Bibliographical Material, Being a Bibliography of Irish Bibliographies and Some Sources of Introduction* (London: Library Association, 1964).

French, Frances-Jane, *The Abbey Theatre Series of Plays* (Dublin: Dolmen Press, 1969).

Greene, David H., and Stephens, Edward M., 'A List of the Published Writings of J. M. Synge', in *J. M. Synge, 1871-1909* (New York: Macmillan, 1959; Collier Books, 1961), p. 308-10.

Levitt, Paul, *A Bibliography of Published Criticism to 1971* (Dublin: Irish University Press, 1974).

Mikhail, E. H., *A Bibliography of Modern Irish Drama 1899-1970* (London: Macmillan, 1972).

Mikhail, E. H., *Dissertations on Anglo-Irish Drama: a Bibliography of Studies 1870-1970* (London: Macmillan, 1973).

Mikhail, E. H., *J. M. Synge: a Bibliography of Criticism* (London: Macmillan, 1975).

Skelton, Robin, 'Chronology and Bibliography', *The Writings of J. M. Synge* (New York: Bobbs-Merrill, 1971), p. 177-84.

Film

Man of Aran (1934), written and directed by Robert Flaherty. [The life of an island family and incidents involving three shark-hunters and three boatmen. Flaherty's narrative places them in dramatic conflict with the raging sea, the film's most important 'character'.]

Audio Recordings

The following are available at the National Sound Archive (29 Exhibition Road, London SW7 2AS), together with recordings of the Abbey Theatre production of The Tinker's Wedding *and* The Well of the Saints *(dir. Hugh Hunt), the National Theatre production of* The Playboy of the Western World *(dir. Bill Bryden), and J. M. Synge, 'a portrait of the dramatist drawn from the memories of his contemporaries'.*

Riders to the Sea and The Shadow of the Glen (Argo RG 223; Spoken Arts SA 743).

The Playboy of the Western World (Audio Forum, BBC SC NO87, with Siobhán McKenna and Éamonn Keane; Caedmon SWC 348, with Siobhán McKenna and Cyril Cusack).

Video Recording

The Playboy of the Western World. A Four Provinces Picture (dir. Brian Desmond Hurst; with Siobhán McKenna as Pegeen Mike, Gary Raymond as Christy, Elspeth March as the Widow Quin, and Liam Redmond as Michael James). VHS PES 39229. Running time 96 mins.

Archive Materials

The Synge Collection of Manuscripts in the Library of Trinity College, Dublin, contains the bulk of Synge's worksheets of plays, notebooks, diaries, and letters. For a detailed catalogue see *The Synge Manuscripts in the Library of Trinity College Dublin* (Dublin, 1971).